High-Performance Deformable Image Registration Algorithms for Manycore Processors

High-Performance Deformable Image Registration Algorithms for Manycore Processors

James Shackleford
Electrical and Computer Engineering Department,
Drexel University

Nagarajan Kandasamy
Electrical and Computer Engineering Department,
Drexel University

Gregory Sharp
Department of Radiation Oncology,
Massachusetts General Hospital

AMSTERDAM • BOSTON • HEIDELBERG • LONDON
NEW YORK • OXFORD • PARIS • SAN DIEGO
SAN FRANCISCO • SINGAPORE • SYDNEY • TOKYO
Morgan Kaufmann is an imprint of Elsevier

Morgan Kaufmann is an imprint of Elsevier
225 Wyman Street, Waltham, MA, 02451, USA

First published 2013

British Library Cataloguing-in-Publication Data
A catalogue record for this book is available from the British Library

Library of Congress Cataloging-in-Publication Data
A catalog record for this book is available from the Library of Congress

ISBN: 978-0-12-407741-6

For information on all MK publications
visit our website at www.mkp.com

This book has been manufactured using Print On Demand technology. Each copy is produced to order and is limited to black ink. The online version of this book will show color figures where appropriate.

ELSEVIER   Book Aid International   Working together to grow libraries in developing countries

www.elsevier.com • www.bookaid.org

CONTENTS

James Shackleford is an assistant professor in the electrical and computer engineering department at Drexel University. Prior to joining Drexel, he was a postdoctoral researcher at Massachusetts General Hospital in the department of radiation oncology. Dr. Shackleford received his Ph.D. from Drexel University in 2011 for his work on GPU-accelerated medical image processing, implemented as part of the plastimatch project (www.plastimatch.org), a deformable registration toolkit for medical images maintained by Drs. Shackleford and Sharp. He has authored a chapter in *NVIDIA's GPU Computing Gems (Emerald Edition)* on the topic of accelerating deformable 3-D image registration using uniform cubic B-splines and this work has also been published as a featured article in the *Physics in Medicine and Biology* journal. His other research interests include nanoscale solid-state device physics.

Nagarajan Kandasamy is an associate professor in the electrical and computer engineering department at Drexel University, where he teaches and conducts research in the area of computer engineering, with specific interests in performance management, parallel computing, embedded systems, fault-tolerant computing, and computer architecture. He received his Ph.D. in 2003 from the University of Michigan. Prof. Kandasamy is a recipient of the National Science Foundation Early Faculty (CAREER) Award, as well as best paper awards at the 2006 and 2008 IEEE International Conferences on Autonomic Computing, for work focusing on the power and performance management of large-scale computer clusters.

Greg Sharp is a computer scientist and medical physicist at Massachusetts General Hospital. He received his Ph.D. in the department of electrical engineering and computer science from the University of Michigan in 2002, and currently holds an appointment of assistant professor of radiation oncology at Harvard Medical School. Prof. Sharp's research interests include medical image computing, image-guided radiation therapy, and motion management.

CHAPTER *1*

Introduction

Information in This Chapter:
- Motivation for multicore CPU/GPU implementations
- Applications of deformable registration
- Algorithmic approaches to deformable registration
- Organization of the book

1.1 INTRODUCTION

The fundamental step for combining three-dimensional (3D) geometric data is *registration*, which is the process of aligning two or more images that capture the geometric structure of the same scene, but in their own relative coordinate frames, into a common coordinate frame. The images themselves can be obtained at different times and from different viewpoints, using similar or different imaging modalities. Here, we focus on *volumetric registration*, where the images are pixel or voxel intensities arranged in a regular grid, and the relative alignment of multiple images must be found. Volumetric registration is often used in biomedical imaging, e.g., to track changes in a patient's anatomy using images taken at different time points or to align stacks of microscopy data in either space or time.

A registration is called *rigid* if the motion or change is limited to global rotations and translations, and is called *deformable* if it includes complex local variations. One of the images is often called the static or reference image and the second image is the moving image, and registration involves spatially transforming the moving image to align with the reference image. When registering medical images, e.g., of a patient's anatomy taken at different time points, one must account for deformation of the anatomy itself due to the patient's breathing, anatomical changes, and so on.

Modern imaging techniques such as computed tomography (CT), positron emission tomography (PET), and magnetic resonance imaging (MRI) provide physicians with 3D image volumes of patient anatomy

High-Performance Deformable Image Registration Algorithms for Manycore Processors.
DOI: http://dx.doi.org/10.1016/B978-0-12-407741-6.00001-3

which convey information instrumental in treating a wide range of afflictions. It is often useful to register one image volume to another to understand how patient anatomy has changed over time or to relate image volumes obtained via different imaging techniques. For example, MRI provides a means of distinguishing soft tissues that are otherwise indiscernible in a transmission-based CT scan, and the recent availability of portable CT scanners inside the operating room has led to the development of new methods of localizing cancerous soft tissue by registering intraoperative CT scans to a preoperative MRI as shown in Figure 1.1, thus allowing for precise tumor localization during the resection procedure.

Efficient and timely processing of 3D data obtained from high-resolution/high-throughput imaging systems requires image analysis algorithms to be significantly accelerated, and registration is no exception. In fact, modern registration algorithms are computationally intensive, and reports of deformable registration algorithms requiring hours to compute for demanding image resolutions and applications are not uncommon (Aylward et al., 2007). Cluster computing is a well-established technique for accelerating image-processing algorithms, since, in many cases, these algorithms can be appropriately parallelized and operations performed independently on different portions of the image. Recent advances in multicore processor design, however, offer new opportunities for truly large-scale and cost-effective parallel computing right at the desk of an individual researcher. For example, CPUs in Intel's Core i7 family have up to six processing cores operating at 3.5 GHz each, and can achieve a peak processing rate of about 100 GLOPs. Graphics Processing Units (GPUs) are considerably more powerful: a modern GPU such as the NVidia C2050 has 448 cores, each operating at 1.1 GHz, and can achieve a peak processing rate of one TFLOP. However, the processing cores on GPUs are considerably simpler in their design than CPU cores. For algorithms that can be parallelized within its programming model, a single GPU offers the computing power equivalent to a small cluster of CPUs.

This book develops highly data-parallel deformable image registration algorithms suitable for use on modern multicore architectures, including GPUs. Reducing the execution time incurred by modern registration algorithms will allow these techniques to be routinely used in both time-sensitive and data-intensive applications.

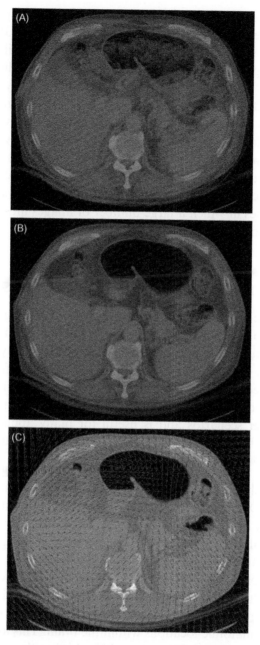

Figure 1.1 Computing organ motion via deformable registration. (A) A preoperative MRI image (in red) super-imposed on an intraoperative CT image (in blue) before deformable registration. (B) The preoperative MRI superimposed on the intraoperative CT after deformable registration. (C) The deformation vector field (in blue) derived by the registration process superimposed on the intraoperative CT scan wherein the vector field quantita-tively describes the organ motion between the CT and MRI scans. (For interpretation of the references to color in this figure legend, the reader is referred to the web version of this book.)

- *Time-sensitive applications*: Many medical-imaging applications are time sensitive. A modern CT scanner can generate 5 GB of raw data in about 20 s, which must be processed and used in applications such as image-guided surgery and image-guided radiotherapy that require very small latencies from imaging to analysis. Examples from computer vision include real-time object recognition in cluttered scenes using range-image registration to solve navigation-related problems in humanoid robots and unmanned vehicles.
- *Data-intensive applications*: Processing large amounts of volumetric data in real time can be done right on a desktop machine equipped with a multicore CPU/GPU, e.g., when constructing statistical anatomical atlases in which a large number of images must be registered with each other.

1.2 APPLICATIONS OF DEFORMABLE IMAGE REGISTRATION

The volumetric registration process consists of aligning two or more 3D images into a common coordinate frame via a deformation vector field. Fusing multiple images in this fashion provides physicians with a more complete understanding of patient anatomy and function. Rigid matching is adequate for serial imaging of the skull, brain, or other rigidly immobilized sites. Deformable registration is appropriate for almost all other scenarios and is useful for many applications within medical research, medical diagnosis, and interventional treatments.

The use of deformable registration has already begun to change medical research practices, especially in the fields of neuroanatomy and brain science. Deformable registration plays an important role in studying a variety of diseases including Alzheimer's disease (Freeborough and Fox, 1998; Scahill et al., 2003; Thompson et al., 2001), schizophrenia (Gharaibeh et al., 2000; Job et al., 2003), and generalized brain development (Thompson et al., 2000). Many of these studies make use of a powerful concept known as brain functional localization (Gholipour et al., 2007), which provides a method of mapping functional information to corresponding anatomic locations within the brain. This allows researchers to correlate patient MRI scans with a brain atlas to improve our understanding of how the brain is damaged by disease.

Deformable registration is also beginning to impact the field of image-guided surgery. For example, neurosurgeons can now track localized deformations within the brain during surgical procedures, thus reducing the amount of unresected tumor (Ferrant et al., 2002; Hartkens et al., 2003). Similar benefits may be observed in surgical operations involving the prostate (Bharatha et al., 2001; Mohamed et al., 2002), heart (Stoyanov, 2005), and the liver (Boctor et al., 2006; Lange et al., 2003) where local complex organ deformation are a common impediment to procedural success. The application of deformable registration to such interventional surgical procedures does, however, carry with it unique challenges. Often, multimodal imaging is required, such as matching an intraoperative ultrasound with preoperative MRI or a preoperative MRI with an intraoperative CT scan. Since such registrations must be performed during active surgical procedures, the time to acquire an accurate solution must be reasonably fast. Additionally, surgical incisions and resections performed prior to intraoperative imaging analysis result in additional deformations that may be difficult to recover algorithmically.

In image-guided radiotherapy, deformable registration is used to improve the geometric and dosimetric accuracy of radiation treatments. Motion due to respiration has a "dose-blurring" effect, which is important for treatments in the lung (Flampouri et al., 2006; Lu et al., 2004; Wang et al., 2005) and liver (Brock et al., 2003; Rietzel et al., 2005; Rohlfing et al., 2004). Day-to-day changes in organ position and shape also affect radiological treatments to the prostate (Foskey et al., 2005) and head and neck regions (Zhang et al., 2007). In addition to improving treatment delivery, deformable registration is also used in treatment verification and treatment response assessment (Brock et al., 2006). Furthermore, deformable registration can be used to construct time-continuous four-dimensional (4D) fields that provide a basis for motion estimation (Mcclelland et al., 2006; Rohkohl et al., 2010) and time-evolution visualization (Brunet et al., 2006), which aids in improving the dosimetric accuracy to tumors within the lung.

1.3 ALGORITHMIC APPROACHES TO DEFORMABLE REGISTRATION

The choice of an image registration method for a particular application is still largely unsettled. There are a variety of deformable image registration algorithms, distinguished by choice of similarity measure, transformation model, and optimization process (Crum et al., 2004; Maintz and Viergever, 1998; Sharp et al., 2010a, 2010b; Zitova and Flusser, 2003). The most popular and successful methods seem to be based on surface matching (Thompson and Toga, 1996), optical flow equations (Thirion, 1998), fluid registration (Christensen et al., 1996), thin-plate splines (Bookstein, 1989), finite-element models (FEMs) (Metaxas, 1997), and B-splines (Rueckert et al., 1999). The involvement of academic researchers in the development of deformable registration methods has resulted in several high-quality open-source software packages. Notable examples include the Insight Segmentation and Registration Toolkit (ITK) (Ibanez et al., 2003), Elastix (Klein et al., 2010), ANTS (Advanced Normalization Tools) providing diffeomorphic registration tools with emphasis on brain mapping (www.picsl.upenn.edu/ANTS/), and IRTK (Image Registration Toolkit) Statistical Parametric, as well as somewhat older packages such as Mapping software (Frackowiak et al., 1997), AIR (Woods et al., 1992), Freesurfer (Fischl et al., 2001), and vtkCISG (Hartkens, 1993).

Though deformable registration has the potential to greatly improve the geometric precision for a variety of medical procedures, modern algorithms are computationally intensive. Consequently, deformable registration algorithms are not commonly accepted into general clinical practice due to their excessive processing time requirements. The fastest family of deformable registration algorithms are based on optical flow methods typically requiring several minutes to compute (Wang et al., 2005), and it is not unusual to hear of B-spline registration algorithms requiring hours to compute (Aylward et al., 2007; Rohde et al., 2003) depending on the specific algorithm implementation, image resolution, and clinical application requirements. However, despite its computational complexity, B-spline-based registration remains popular due to its flexibility and robustness in providing the ability to perform both unimodal and multimodal registrations. In other words, B-spline-based registration is capable of registering two images obtained via the same imaging method (unimodal registration) as well as images obtained via differing imaging methods (multimodal registration). Consequently, surgical operations benefiting from CT to MRI registration may be routinely performed once multimodal B-spline-based registration can be performed with adequate speed.

A key element in accelerating medical-imaging algorithms, including deformable registration, is the use of parallel processing. In many cases, images may be partitioned into computationally independent subregions and subsequently farmed out to be processed in parallel. The most prominent example of this approach is the use of a solver such as PETSc (http://www.mcs.anl.gov/petsc). The PETSc library is a suite of data structures and parallel routines for partial differential equations (PDEs) that are accelerated using a combination of Message Passing Interface (MPI), shared memory pthreads, and GPU programming. Parallel MPI-based implementations of the FEM-based registration method using PETsc have been demonstrated and benchmarked by Warfield et al. (2000, 2005) and Sermesant et al. (2003). The overall approach is to first parallelize the appropriate algorithmic steps (e.g., the displacement field estimation), partition the image data into small sets, and then process each set independently on a computer within the cluster.

While cluster computing is a well-established technique for accelerating image computing algorithms, recent advances in multicore processor design offer new opportunities for truly large-scale and cost-effective parallel computing on a single chip. The cell processor and GPUs are two examples of many-core processors designed specifically to support the single chip parallel computing paradigm. These processors have a large number of arithmetic units on chip, far more than any general-purpose microprocessor, making them well suited for high-performance parallel-processing tasks. There has been a significant amount of recent research aimed at accelerating a range of image computing algorithms, including image reconstruction, registration, and fusion using these new hardware platforms, especially GPUs, and we refer the interested reader to the following two recent articles and the references therein for a good survey of ongoing research in this area. Pratx and Xing (2011) survey applications of GPU computing in the major areas of medical physics: image reconstruction, dose calculation and treatment plan optimization, and image processing. Shams (2010) provides a survey of registration algorithms for medical images, both rigid and deformable, that have been implemented using high-performance computing architectures including multicore CPUs and GPUs.

1.4 ORGANIZATION OF CHAPTERS

This book aims to provide the reader with an understanding of how to design and implement deformable registration algorithms suitable for execution on multicore CPUs and GPUs, focusing on two widely used algorithms: demons (optical flow) and B-spline-based registration. The GPU kernels are implemented using Compute Unified Device Architecture (CUDA), the programming interface used by NVidia GPUs, and the multicore CPU versions are developed using OpenMP. The algorithms discussed in the subsequent chapters have been implemented and validated as part of the Plastimatch project (http://

www.plastimatch.org), a suite of open-source, high-performance algorithms for image computing being developed by the authors (Shackleford et al., 2010a, 2010b, 2012a, 2012b; Sharp et al., 2007, 2010a, 2010b).

Chapter 2 provides an overview of the unimodal B-spline registration algorithm and subsequently introduces a grid-alignment scheme for improving the algorithm's computation speed for both single and multicore architectures. Using the grid-alignment scheme as a foundation, a high-performance multicore algorithm is developed and described in detail. The fundamental concepts of image-similarity scoring, vector field evolution, and B-spline parameterization are covered in depth. Additionally, aspects of the CUDA programming model relevant to implementing the B-spline deformable registration algorithm on modern GPU hardware are introduced and discussed, and a highly parallel GPU implementation is developed. Finally, the single-core CPU, multicore CPU, and many-core GPU-based implementations are benchmarked for performance and registration quality using synthetic CT images as well as thoracic CT image volumes.

Chapter 3 describes how the B-spline registration algorithm may be extended to perform multimodal image registration by utilizing the mutual information (MI) similarity metric. Modifications to the algorithm structure and the data flow presented in Chapter 2 are discussed in detail, and strategies for accelerating these new algorithmic additions are explored. Specific attention is directed toward developing memory-efficient and data-parallel methods of constructing the marginal and joint image-intensity histograms, since these data structures are key to successfully performing the MI-based registration. The impact of the MI similarity metric on the analytic formalism driving the vector field evolution is covered in depth. The partial volume interpolation method is also introduced; dictating how the image-intensity histogram data structures evolve with the vector field evolution. Multicore implementations are benchmarked for performance using synthetic image volumes. Finally, registration quality is assessed using examples of multimodal thoracic MRI to CT deformable registration.

Chapter 4 develops an analytic method for constraining the evolution of the deformation vector field that seamlessly integrates into both unimodal and multimodal B-spline-based registration algorithms. Although the registration methods presented in Chapters 2 and 3 generate vector fields describing how best to transform one image to match the other, there is no guarantee that these transformations will be physically valid. Image registration is an ill-posed problem in that it lacks a unique solution to the vector deformation field, and consequently, the solution may describe a physical deformation that did not or could not have occurred. However, by imposing constraints on the character of the vector field, it is possible to guide its evolution toward physically meaningful solutions; in other words, the ill-posed problem is regularized. This chapter provides the analytic mathematical formalism required to impose second-order smoothness upon the deformation vector field in a faster and more efficient fashion than numerically based central differencing methods. Furthermore, we show that such analytically-derived matrix operators may be applied directly to the B-spline parameterization of the vector field to achieve the desired physically meaningful solutions. Single and multicore CPU implementations are developed and discussed and the performance for both implementations is investigated with respect to the numerical method in terms of execution-time overhead, and the quality of the analytic implementations is investigated via a thoracic MRI to CT case study.

Chapter 5 deals with optical flow methods that describe the registration problem as a set of flow equations, under the assumption that image intensities are constant between views. The most common variant is the "demons algorithm," which combines a stabilized vector field estimation algorithm with Gaussian regularization. The algorithm is iterative and alternates between solving the flow equations and regularization. We describe data-parallel designs for the demons deformable registration algorithm, suitable for use on a GPU. Streaming versions of these algorithms are implemented using the CUDA programming environment.

Free and open-source software is playing an increasingly important role throughout society. Free software provides a common economic good by reducing duplicated effort and advances science by promoting the open exchange of ideas. Chapter 6 introduces the Plastimatch open software suite, which implements a variety of useful tools for high-performance image computing. These tools include cone-beam CT reconstruction, rigid and deformable image registration, digitally reconstructed radiographs, and DICOM-RT file exchange.

REFERENCES

Aylward, S., Jomier, J., Barre, S., Davis, B., Ibanez, L., 2007. Optimizing ITK’s registration methods for multi-processor, shared-memory systems. MICCAI Open Source and Open Data Workshop. Brisbane, Australia.

Bharatha, A., Hirose, M., Hata, N., Warfield, S.K., Ferrant, M., Zou, K.H., et al., 2001. Evaluation of three-dimensional finite element-based deformable registration of pre- and intraoperative prostate imaging. Med. Phys. 28 (12), 2551–2560.

Boctor, E., deOliveira, M., Choti, M., Ghanem, R., Taylor, R., Hager, G., et al., 2006. Ultrasound monitoring of tissue ablation via deformation model and shape priors. International Conference on Medical Image Computing and Computer-Assisted Intervention, Copenhagen, Denmark., pp. 405–412.

Bookstein, F., 1989. Principal warps: thin-plate splines and the decomposition of deformations. IEEE Trans. Pattern Anal. Mach. Intell. 11 (6), 567–585.

Brock, K., Balter, J., Dawson, L., Kessler, M., Meyer, C., 2003. Automated generation of a four-dimensional model of the liver using warping and mutual information. Med. Phys. 30 (6), 1128–1133.

Brock, K., Dawson, L., Sharpe, M., Moseley, D., Jaffray, D., 2006. Feasibility of a novel deformable image registration technique to facilitate classification, targeting, and monitoring of tumor and normal tissue. Int. J. Radiat. Oncol. Biol. Phys. 64 (4), 1245–1254.

Brunet, T., Nowak, K., Gleicher, M., 2006. Integrating dynamic deformations into interactive volume visualization. Eurographics/IEEE VGTC Conference on Visualization. Lisbon, Portugal., pp. 219–226.

Christensen, G., Rabbitt, R., Miller, M., 1996. Deformable templates using large deformation kinematics. IEEE Trans. Image Process. 5 (10), 1435–1447.

Crum, W., Hartkens, T., Hill, D., 2004. Non-rigid image registration: theory and practice. Br. J. Radiol. 77, S140–S153.

Ferrant, M., Nabavi, A., Macq, B., Black, P., Jolesz, F., Kikinis, R., et al., 2002. Serial registration of intra-operative MR images of the brain. Med. Image Anal. 6 (4), 337–360.

Fischl, B., Liu, A., Dale, A., 2001. Automated manifold surgery: constructing geometrically accurate and topologically correct models of the human cerebral cortex. IEEE Trans. Med. Imaging 20 (1), 70–80.

Flampouri, S., Jiang, S., Sharp, G., Wolfgang, J., Patel, A., Choi, N., 2006. Estimation of the delivered patient dose in lung IMRT treatment based on deformable registration of 4D-CT data and Monte Carlo simulations. Phys. Med. Biol. 51 (11), 2763–2779.

Foskey, M., Davis, B., Goyal, L., Chang, S., Chaney, E., Strehl, N., et al., 2005. Large deformation three-dimensional image registration in image-guided radiation therapy. Phys. Med. Biol. 50 (24), 5869–5892.

Frackowiak, R., Friston, K., Frith, C., Dolan, R., Mazziotta, J. (Eds.), 1997. Human Brain Function. Academic Press, Waltham, MA, USA.

Freeborough, P., Fox, N., 1998. Modeling brain deformations in Alzheimer disease by fluid registration of serial 3D MR images. J. Comput. Assist. Tomogr. 22 (5), 838–843.

Gharaibeh, W., Rohlf, F., Slice, D., DeLisi, L., 2000. A geometric morphometric assessment of change in midline brain structural shape following a first episode of schizophrenia. Biol. Psychiatry 48 (5), 398–405.

Gholipour, A., Kehtarnavaz, N., Briggs, R., Devous, M., Gopinath, K., 2007. Brain functional localization: a survey of image registration techniques. IEEE Trans. Med. Imaging 26 (4), 427–451.

Hartkens, T., 1993. Measuring, Analyzing, and Visualizing Brain Deformation Using Non-Rigid Registration. PhD thesis, King's College, London.

Hartkens, T., Hill, D.L., Castellano-Smith, A.D, Hawkes, D.J., Maurer Jr., C.R., Martin, T., et al., 2003. Measurement and analysis of brain deformation during neurosurgery. IEEE Trans. Med. Imaging 22 (1), 82–92.

Ibanez, L., Schroeder, W., Ng, L., Cates, J., 2003. The ITK Software Guide. Kitware, Inc., Clifton Park, NY, USA, <http://www.itk.org/ItkSoftwareGuide.pdf>.

Job, D., Whalley, H., McConnell, S., Glabus, M., Johnstone, E., Lawrie, S., 2003. Voxel-based morphometry of grey matter densities in subjects at high risk of schizophrenia. Schizophr. Res. 64 (1), 1–13.

Klein, S., Staring, M., Murphy, K., Viergever, M.A., Pluim, J.P.W., 2010. Elastix: a toolbox for intensity based medical image registration. IEEE Trans. Med. Imaging 29 (1), 196–205.

Lange, T., Eulenstein, S., Hunerbein, M., Schlag, P., 2003. Vessel-based non-rigid registration of MR/CT and 3D ultrasound for navigation in liver surgery. Comput. Aided Surg. 8 (5), 228–240.

Lu, W., Chen, M., Olivera, G., Ruchala, K., Mackie, T., 2004. Fast free-form deformable registration via calculus of variations. Phys. Med. Biol. 49 (14), 3067–3087.

Maintz, J., Viergever, M., 1998. A survey of medical image registration. Med. Image Anal. 2 (1), 1–37.

McClelland, J.R., Blackall, J.M., Tarte, S., Chandler, A.C., Hughes, S., Ahmad, S., et al., 2006. A continuous 4D motion model from multiple respiratory cycles for use in lung radiotherapy. Med. Phys. 33 (9), 3348–3359.

Metaxas, D., 1997. Physics-Based Deformable Models: Applications to Computer Vision, Graphics and Medical Imaging. Kluwer Academic Publishers, Norwell, MA, USA.

Mohamed, A., Davatzikos, C., Taylor, R., 2002. A combined statistical and biomechanical model for estimation of intra-operative prostate deformation. International Conference on Medical Image Computing and Computer-Assisted Intervention. Tokyo, Japan., pp. 452–460.

Pratx, G., Xing, L., 2011. GPU computing in medical physics: a review. Med. Phys. 38 (5), 2685–2698.

Rietzel, E., Chen, G., Choi, N., Willet, C., 2005. Four-dimensional image-based treatment planning: target volume segmentation and dose calculation in the presence of respiratory motion. Int. J. Radiat. Oncol. Biol. Phys. 61 (5), 1535–1550.

Rohde, G., Aldroubi, A., Dawant, B., 2003. The adaptive bases algorithm for intensity based nonrigid image registration. IEEE Trans. Med. Imaging 22 (11), 1470–1479.

Rohkohl, C., Lauritsch, G., Biller, L., Prümmer, M., Boese, J., Rohkohl, C., et al., 2010. Interventional 4-D motion estimation and reconstruction of cardiac vasculature without motion periodicity assumption. Med. Image Anal. 14 (5), 687–694.

Rohlfing, T., Maurer, C., O'Dell, W., Zhong, J., 2004. Modeling liver motion and deformation during the respiratory cycle using intensity-based nonrigid registration of gated MR images. Med. Phys. 31 (3), 427–432.

Rueckert, D., Sonoda, L.I., Hayes, C., Hill, D.L., Leach, M.O., Hawkes, D.J., et al., 1999. Nonrigid registration using free-form deformations: application to breast MR images. IEEE Trans. Med. Imaging 18 (8), 712–721.

Scahill, R.I., Frost, C., Jenkins, R., Whitwell, J.L., Rossor, M.N., Fox, N.C., et al., 2003. A longitudinal study of brain volume changes in normal aging using serial registered magnetic resonance imaging. Arch. Neurol. 60 (7), 989–994.

Sermesant, Clatz, M.O., Li, Z., Lantéri, S., Delingette, H., Ayache, N., 2003. A parallel implementation of non-rigid registration using a volumetric biomechanical model. WBIR Workshop, Springer-Verlag, Philadelphia, PA, USA, pp. 398–407.

Shackleford, J., Kandasamy, N., Sharp, G., 2010a. On developing B-spline registration algorithms for multi-core processors. Phys. Med. Biol. 55 (21), 6329–6352.

Shackleford, J., Kandasamy, N., Sharp, G., 2010b. Deformable volumetric registration using B-splines. In: Hwu, W.-M. (Ed.), GPU Computing Gems, 4. Elsevier, Amsterdam, The Netherlands.

Shackleford, J., Yang, Q., Louren, A., Shusharina, N., Kandasamy, N., Sharp, G.,2012a. Analytic regularization of uniform cubic < mac_ah > B-spline < /mac_ah > deformation fields. International Conference on Medical Image Computing and Computer Assisted Intervention, Nice, France, vol. 15 (Part 2), pp. 122–129.

Shackleford, J., Kandasamy, N., Sharp, G., 2012b. Accelerating MI-based B-spline registration using CUDA enabled GPUs. MICCAI 2012 Data- and Compute-Intensive Clinical and Translational Imaging Applications (DICTA-MICCAI) Workshop, Nice, France.

Shams, R., Sadeghi, P., Kennedy, R.A., Hartley, R.I., 2010. A survey of medical image registration on multi-core and the GPU. IEEE Signal Process. Mag. 27 (2), 50–60.

Sharp, G., Kandasamy, N., Singh, H., Folkert, M., 2007. GPU-based streaming architectures for fast cone-beam CT image reconstruction and demons deformable registration. Phys. Med. Biol. 52 (19), 5771–5783.

Sharp, G., Peroni, M., Li, R., Shackleford, J., Kandasamy, N., 2010a. Evaluation of Plastimatch B-spline registration on the empire10 data set. Medical Image Analysis for the Clinic: A Grand Challenge, MICCAI Workshop, Beijing, China, pp. 99–108.

Sharp, G., Li, R., Wolfgang, J., Chen, G., Peroni, M., Spadea, M., et al., 2010b. Plastimatch: an open source software suite for radiotherapy image processing. International Conference on Computers Radiation Therapy (ICCR), Amsterdam, The Netherlands.

Stoyanov, D., Mylonas, G., Deligianni, F., Darzi, A., Yang, G., 2005. Soft-tissue motion tracking and structure estimation for robotic assisted MIS procedures. International Conference on Medical Image Computing and Computer-Assisted Intervention. Palm Springs, California, USA, pp. 139–146.

Thirion, J., 1998. Image matching as a diffusion process: an analogy with Maxwell's demons. Med. Image Anal. 2 (3), 243–260.

Thompson, P., Toga, A., 1996. A surface-based technique for warping three-dimensional images of the brain. IEEE Trans. Med. Imaging 15 (4), 402–417.

Thompson, P., Giedd, J., Woods, R., MacDonald, D., Evans, A., Toga, A., 2000. Growth patterns in the developing human brain detected using continuum-mechanical tensor mapping. Nature 404 (6774), 190–193.

Thompson, P.M, Mega, M.S., Woods, R.P., Zoumalan, C.I., Lindshield, C.J., Blanton, R.E., et al., 2001. Cortical change in Alzheimer's disease detected with a disease-specific population-based brain atlas. Cereb. Cortex 11 (1), 1–16.

Wang, H., Dong, L., O'Daniel, H., Mohan, R., Garden, A.S., Ang, K.K., et al., 2005. Validation of an accelerated 'demons' algorithm for deformable image registration in radiation therapy. Phys. Med. Biol. 50 (12), 2887–2905.

Warfield, S., Ferrant, M., Gallez, X., Nabavi, A., Jolesz, F., Kikinis, R., 2000. Real-time bio-mechanical simulation of volumetric brain deformation for image guided neurosurgery. Supercomputing. Article 23, 1–16.

Warfield, S.K, Haker, S.J., Talos, I.F., Kemper, C.A., Weisenfeld, N., Mewes, A.U., et al., 2005. Capturing intraoperative deformations: research experience at Brigham and Women's hospital. Med. Image Anal. 9 (2), 145–162.

Woods, R., Cherry, S., Mazziotta, J., 1992. Rapid automated algorithm for aligning and reslicing PET images. J. Comput. Assist. Tomogr. 16 (4), 620–633.

Zhang, T., Chi, Y., Meldolesi, E., Yan, D., 2007. Automatic delineation of on-line head-and-neck computed tomography images: toward on-line adaptive radiotherapy. Int. J. Radiat. Oncol. Biol. Phys. 68 (2), 522–530.

Zitova, B., Flusser, J., 2003. Image registration methods: a survey. Image Vis. Comput. 21, 977–1000.

CHAPTER 2

Unimodal B-Spline Registration

Information in This Chapter:
- Overview of B-spline registration
- Optimized implementation of the B-spline interpolation operation
- Computation of the cost function gradient and optimization of the B-spline coefficients
- Design of GPU kernels to perform the interpolation and gradient calculations
- Performance evaluation

2.1 INTRODUCTION

B-spline registration is a method of deformable registration that uses B-spline curves to define a continuous deformation field that maps each and every voxel in a moving image to a corresponding voxel within a fixed or reference image (Rueckert et al., 1999). An optimal deformation field accurately describes how the voxels in the moving image have been displaced with respect to their original positions in the fixed image. Naturally, this assumes that the two images are of the same scene taken at different times using similar or different imaging modalities. This chapter deals with *unimodal registration* which is the process of matching images obtained via the same imaging modality. Figure 2.1 shows an example of deformable registration of two 3D CT images using B-splines, where registration is performed between an inhaled lung image and an exhaled image taken at two different times. Prior to registration, the image difference shown is quite large, highlighting the motion of the diaphragm and pulmonary vessels during breathing. Registration is performed to generate the vector or displacement field. After registration, the image difference is much smaller, demonstrating that the registration has successfully matched tissues of similar density.

In the case of B-spline registration, the dense deformation field can be parameterized by a sparse set of control points which are uniformly

High-Performance Deformable Image Registration Algorithms for Manycore Processors.
DOI: http://dx.doi.org/10.1016/B978-0-12-407741-6.00002-5

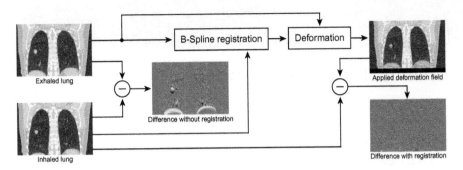

Figure 2.1 Deformable registration of two 3D CT volumes. Images of an inhaled lung and an exhaled lung taken at different times from the same patient serve as the fixed and moving images, respectively. The registration algorithm iteratively deforms the moving image in an attempt to minimize the intensity difference between the images. The final result is a vector field describing how voxels in the moving image should be shifted in order to make it match the fixed image. The difference between the fixed and moving images with and without registration is also shown.

distributed throughout the moving image's voxel grid. This results in the formation of two grids that are aligned with one another: a dense voxel grid and a sparse control point grid. Individual voxel movement between the two images is parameterized in terms of the coefficient values provided by these control points, and the displacement vectors are obtained via interpolation of these control point coefficients using piecewise continuous B-spline basis functions. Registration of images can then be posed as a numerical optimization problem wherein the spline coefficients are refined iteratively until the warped moving image closely matches the fixed image. Gradient descent optimization is often used, meaning either analytic or numeric gradient estimates must be available to the optimizer after each iteration. This requires that we evaluate (i) a cost function corresponding to a given set of spline coefficients that quantifies the similarity between the fixed and moving images and (ii) the change in this cost function with respect to the coefficient values at each individual control point which we will refer to as the cost function gradient. The registration process then becomes one of iteratively defining coefficients, performing B-spline interpolation, evaluating the cost function, calculating the cost function gradient for each control point, and performing gradient descent optimization to generate the next set of coefficients.

The above-described process has two time-consuming steps: B-spline interpolation, wherein a coarse array of B-spline coefficients is taken as the input and a fine array of displacement values is computed as the output defining the vector field from the moving image to the reference image, and the cost function gradient computation that requires evaluating the partial derivatives of the cost function with respect to each spline-coefficient value. Recent work has focused on accelerating these steps within the overall registration process using multicore processors. For example, the authors Rohlfing et al. (2003), Rohrer et al. (2008), Zheng et al. (2009), and Saxena et al. (2010) have developed parallel deformable registration algorithms using mutual information between the images as the similarity measure. Results reported by Zheng et al. (2009) for B-splines show a speedup of $n/2$ for n processors compared to a sequential implementation; two $512 \times 512 \times 459$ images are registered in 12 min using a cluster of 10 computers, each with a 3.4-GHz CPU, compared to 50 min for a sequential program. Rohfling et al. (2003) present a parallel design and implementation of a B-spline registration algorithm based on mutual information for shared-memory multiprocessor machines. Rohrer et al. (2008) describe a design for the Cell processor and a GPU-based design is discussed in Saxena et al. (2010).

This chapter describes how to develop GPU-based designs to accelerate both steps in the B-spline registration process, and its main contribution with respect to the state of the art lies in the design of the second step: the cost function gradient computation. We show how to optimize the GPU-based designs to achieve coalesced accesses to GPU global memory, a high compute to memory access ratio (number of floating point calculations performed for each memory access), and efficient use of shared memory. The resulting design, therefore, computes and aggregates the large amount of intermediate values needed to obtain the gradient very efficiently and can process large data sets.

We follow a systematic approach to accelerating B-spline registration algorithms. First, we develop a fast reference (sequential) implementation by developing a grid-alignment technique and accompanying data structure that greatly reduces redundant computation in the registration algorithm. We then show how to identify the data parallelism of the grid-aligned algorithm and how to restructure it to fit the single instruction, multiple data (SIMD) model, necessary to effectively utilize the large number of processing cores available in modern GPUs. The SIMD model can exploit the fine-grain parallelism present in registration algorithms, wherein operations can be performed on individual voxels in parallel. For complex spline-based algorithms, however, there are many ways of structuring the same algorithm within the SIMD model, making the problem quite challenging. A number of SIMD versions must therefore be developed and their performance analyzed to discover the optimal implementation. We introduce a carefully optimized implementation that avoids redundant computations while exhibiting regular memory access patterns that are highly conducive to the GPU's memory architecture. We also evaluate other design options with speedup implications such as using a lookup table (LUT) on the GPU to store precomputed spline parameterization data versus computing this information on the fly.

Finally, single-core CPU, multicore CPU, and many-core GPU-based implementations are benchmarked for performance as well as registration quality. The NVidia Tesla C1060 and 680 GTX GPU platforms are used for the GPU versions. Though speedup varies by image size, in the best case, the 680 GTX achieves a speedup of 39 times over the reference implementation and the multicore CPU algorithm achieves a speedup of 8 times over the reference when executed on eight CPU cores. Furthermore, the registration quality achieved by the GPU is nearly identical to that of the CPU in terms of the RMS differences between the vector fields.

2.2 OVERVIEW OF B-SPLINE REGISTRATION

The B-spline deformable registration algorithm maps each and every voxel in a fixed image S to a corresponding voxel in a moving image M. This mapping is described by a deformation field $\vec{\nu}$, which is defined at each and every voxel within the fixed image. An optimal deformation field accurately describes how the voxels in M have been displaced with respect to their original positions in S and finding this deformation field is an iterative process. Also, as noted in the introduction, B-spline interpolation and gradient computation are the two most time-consuming stages within the overall registration process, and so we will focus on accelerating these stages using a grid-alignment scheme and accompanying data structures.

2.2.1 Using B-Splines to Represent the Deformation Field

The dense deformation field $\vec{\nu}$ is parameterized by a sparse set of control points, which are uniformly distributed throughout the fixed image's voxel grid. This results in the formation of two grids that are aligned to one another: a dense voxel grid and a sparse control point grid. In this scheme, the control point grid partitions the voxel grid into many equally sized regions called *tiles*. A spline curve is a type of continuous curve defined by a sparse set of discrete control points. Generally speaking, the number of control points required for each dimension is $n + 1$, where n is the order of the employed spline curve. Since we are working with cubic B-splines, we require 4 control points in each dimension, which results in 64 (4^3) control points for each tile. The deformation field at any given voxel within a tile is computed by utilizing the 64 control points in the immediate vicinity of the tile. Furthermore, because we are working in three dimensions, three coefficients (P_x, P_y, P_z) are associated with each control point, one for each dimension. Mathematically, the x-component of the deformation field for a voxel located at coordinates (x, y, z) in the fixed image can be described as

$$\nu_x(\vec{x}) = \sum_{i=0}^{3} \sum_{j=0}^{3} \sum_{k=0}^{3} \beta_i(u)\beta_j(v)\beta_k(w)P_x(l, m, n), \qquad (2.1)$$

where $\beta(.)$ are the spline basis functions obtained as follows. Let $N_x, N_y,$ and N_z denote the distance between control points in terms of voxels in the $x, y,$ and z directions, respectively. The volume is therefore segmented by the control point grid into many equal-sized tiles, each of dimension $N_x \times N_y \times N_z$ voxels. Then, the 3D coordinate of the tile within which the voxel $\vec{\nu}$ falls is given by

$$\left\lfloor \frac{x}{N_x} \right\rfloor - 1, \quad \left\lfloor \frac{y}{N_y} \right\rfloor - 1, \quad \left\lfloor \frac{z}{N_z} \right\rfloor - 1 \qquad (2.2)$$

and the 64 control points influencing the voxels within the tile are indexed via $l, m,$ and n, where

$$l = \left\lfloor \frac{x}{N_x} - 1 + i \right\rfloor, \quad m = \left\lfloor \frac{y}{N_y} - 1 + j \right\rfloor, \quad n = \left\lfloor \frac{z}{N_z} - 1 + k \right\rfloor \qquad (2.3)$$

The local coordinates (u, v, w) of the voxel within its housing tile are

$$u = \frac{x}{N_x} - \left\lfloor \frac{x}{N_x} \right\rfloor, \quad v = \frac{y}{N_y} - \left\lfloor \frac{y}{N_y} \right\rfloor, \quad w = \frac{z}{N_z} - \left\lfloor \frac{z}{N_z} \right\rfloor \qquad (2.4)$$

which are normalized between $[0, 1]$. Finally, the uniform cubic B-spline basis function β_l along the x-direction is given by

$$\beta_i(u) = \begin{cases} \dfrac{(1-u)^3}{6} & :i = 0 \\[2mm] \dfrac{3u^3 - 6u^2 + 4}{6} & :i = 1 \\[2mm] \dfrac{-3u^3 + 3u^2 + 3u + 1}{6} & :i = 2 \\[2mm] \dfrac{u^3}{6} & :i = 3 \end{cases} \tag{2.5}$$

and similarly for β_m and β_n along the y and z directions, respectively.

Figure 2.2 visualizes the computation of the deformation field within a single tile for a two-dimensional image. Because this example is 2D, only 16 control points are required to compute the deformation field for

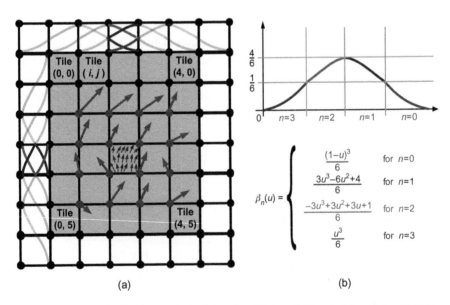

(a)   (b)

Figure 2.2 Graphical example of computing the deformation field from B-spline coefficients in two dimensions. (A) The 16 control points needed to compute the deformation field within the highlighted tile are shown in blue. The purple arrows represent the deformation vectors associated with each voxel within the tile. (B) Uniform cubic B-spline basis function plotted (top) and written as a piecewise algebraic equation (bottom). (For interpretation of the references to color in this figure legend, the reader is referred to the web version of this book.)

any given tile; the 16 needed to compute the deformation field within the highlighted tile have been drawn in grey, whereas all the other control points are drawn in black. Each of these control points has associated with it two coefficients, (P_x, P_y), which are depicted as the x and y components of the larger arrows. The B-spline basis functions β_l and β_m have been superimposed on the grid's x-axis and y-axis, respectively, to aid understanding. Pieces of the B-spline basis functions irrelevant to the highlighted tile's deformation field computation have been faded. The smaller arrows represent the deformation field, which is obtained by computing ν_x and ν_y for each voxel within the tile. The 3D case is similar but requires the additional computation of ν_z at each voxel.

A straightforward implementation of Eq. (2.1) to compute the displacement vector $\vec{\nu}$ for a single voxel requires 192 computations of the cubic polynomial B-spline basis function β as well as 192 multiplications and 63 additions. However, many of these calculations are redundant and can be eliminated by implementing a data structure that exploits symmetrical features that emerge as a result of the grid alignment, making the implementation of Eq. (2.1) much faster (Shackleford et al., 2010). To see how this can be done, let us consider the example shown in Figure 2.3A. By aligning the voxel grid with a uniformly spaced control grid, the image volume becomes partitioned into many equal-sized tiles. In the example, the control grid partitions the voxel grid into 6×5 tiles. The vector field at any given voxel within a tile is influenced by the 16 control points in the tile's immediate vicinity and the value of the B-spline basis function product evaluated at the voxel, which depends only on the voxel's local coordinates (or offset) within the tile. Notice that the two marked voxels in Figure 2.3A, while residing at different locations within the image, both possess the same offsets within their respective tiles. This results in the B-spline basis function product yielding identical values when evaluated at these two voxels. This property allows us to precompute all relevant B-spline basis function products once instead of recomputing the evaluation for each individual tile. In general, aligning the control and voxel grids allows us to perform the following optimizations when performing the interpolation operation using cubic B-splines:

- All voxels residing within a single tile use the same set of 64 control points to compute their respective displacement vectors. So, for each tile in the volume, the corresponding set of control point indices can

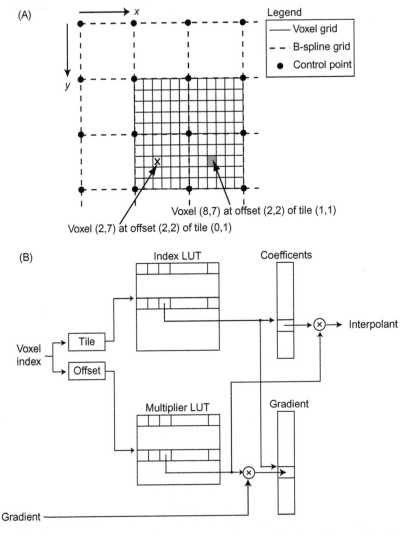

Figure 2.3 (A) A portion of a 2D image showing a B-spline control point grid superimposed upon an aligned voxel grid. Since both the marked voxel and the grayed voxel are located at the same relative offset within their respective tiles, both voxels will use the same $\beta_l(u)\beta_m(v)$. (B) For aligned grids, LUTs can accelerate deformable registration computations by eliminating redundant computations.

be precomputed and stored in an LUT, called the *Index LUT*. These indices then serve as pointers to a table containing the corresponding B-spline coefficients.

- For a tile of dimension $N_w = N_x \times N_y \times N_z$, the number of $\beta(u)\beta(v)\beta(w)$ combinations is limited to N_w values. Furthermore, two voxels belonging to different tiles but possessing the same normalized coordinates (u, v, w) within their respective tiles will be subject to identical $\beta(u)\beta(v)\beta(w)$ products. Therefore, we can precompute these values for all valid normalized coordinate combinations $(u, v, \text{and } w)$ and store the results into a LUT called the *Multiplier LUT*.

Figure 2.3B shows the complete data structure required to support the above-described optimizations. For each voxel, its absolute coordinate (x, y, z) within the volume is used to calculate the tile number that the voxel falls within as well as the voxel's relative coordinates within that tile using Eqs. (2.2) and (2.4), respectively. The tile number is used to query the *Index LUT*, which provides the coefficient values associated with the 64 control points influencing the voxel's interpolation calculation. The voxel's relative coordinates (u, v, w) within the tile determine its index within $[0, N_w]$, which is used to retrieve the appropriate precomputed $\beta(u)\beta(v)\beta(w)$ product from the *Multiplier LUT*. Computing ν_x, the x-component of the displacement vector for the voxel, therefore, requires looping through the 64 entries of each LUT, fetching the associated values, multiplying, and accumulating. Similar computations are required to obtain ν_y and ν_z. The LUTs are stored in CPU cache or in the texture unit on the GPU, thereby achieving very fast lookup times.

2.2.2 Computing the Cost Function

Once the displacement vector field is generated as per Eq. (2.1), it is used to deform each voxel in the moving image. Trilinear interpolation is used to determine the value of voxels mapping to noninteger grid coordinates. Once deformed, the moving image is compared to the fixed image in terms of a cost function. Recall that a better registration results in a mapping between the fixed and moving images causing them to appear more similar. As a result, the cost function is sometimes also referred to as a *similarity metric*. The unimodal registration process matches images using the *sum of squared differences* (SSD) cost function which is computed once per iteration by accumulating the square of the intensity difference between the fixed image S and the deformed moving image M as

$$C = \frac{1}{N}\sum\sum\sum (S(x, y, z) - M(x + \nu_x, y + \nu_y, z + \nu_z))^2, \qquad (2.6)$$

where N denotes the total number of voxels in the moving image M after the application of the deformation field $\vec{\nu}$.

2.2.3 Optimizing the B-Spline Coefficients

While evaluating the cost function provides a metric for determining the quality of a registration for a given set of coefficients, it provides no insight as to how we can optimize the coefficients to yield an even better registration. However, by taking the derivative of the cost function C with respect to the B-spline coefficients P, we can determine how the cost function changes as the coefficients change. This provides us with the means to conduct an intelligent search for coefficients that cause the cost function to decrease and, thus, obtain a better registration. Such a method of optimization is known as *gradient descent* and, in this context, the derivative of the cost function is referred to as the *cost function gradient*. As we move along the cost function gradient, the cost function will decrease until we reach a global (or local) minimum. Though there are more sophisticated methods of optimization, a simple method would be to use

$$P_{i+1} = P_i - a_i \frac{\partial C}{\partial P_i}, \quad i = 1, 2, 3, \ldots \tag{2.7}$$

to iteratively tune P, the vector comprising the P_x, P_y, and P_z B-spline coefficients. Here, i denotes the iteration number and a_i is a scalar gain factor that regulates how fast we descend along the gradient.

To compute the gradient for a control point at grid coordinates (κ, λ, μ) we begin by using the chain rule to decompose the expression into two terms as

$$\frac{\partial C}{\partial P_{\kappa, \lambda, \mu}} = \frac{1}{N} \sum_{(x,y,z)} \frac{\partial C}{\partial \vec{v}(x, y, z)} \frac{\partial \vec{v}(x, y, z)}{\partial P} \tag{2.8}$$

where the summation is performed over all voxels (x, y, z) contained within the 64 tiles found in the control point's local support region (Kybic and Unser, 2003). This decomposition allows us to evaluate the cost function gradient's dependencies on the cost function and spline coefficients separately. The first term describes how the cost function changes with the deformation field, and since the deformation field is defined at every voxel, so is $\partial C / \partial v$. It depends only on the cost function and is independent of the type of spline parameterization employed. The second term describes how the deformation field changes with respect to the control point coefficients and can be found by simply taking the derivative of Eq. (2.1) with respect to P as

$$\frac{\partial \vec{\nu}(x,y,z)}{\partial P} = \sum_{l=0}^{3}\sum_{m=0}^{3}\sum_{n=0}^{3} \beta_l(u)\beta_m(v)\beta_n(w) \tag{2.9}$$

We find that this term is dependent only on the B-spline basis functions. So, it will remain constant over all optimization iterations. This allows us to precompute and store Eq. (2.9) for each voxel coordinate prior to the optimization process. Note also, that the values generated by Eq. (2.9) are already available via the *Multiplier LUT*.

When using the SSD as the cost function, the first term of Eq. (2.8) can be rewritten in terms of the moving image's spatial gradient $\nabla M(x,y,z)$ as

$$\frac{\partial C}{\partial \vec{\nu}(x,y,z)} = 2 \times \left[S(x,y,z) - M(x+\nu_x, y+\nu_y, z+\nu_z)\right]\nabla M(x,y,z)$$

$$\tag{2.10}$$

Equation (2.10) depends on the intensity values of the static and moving images, S and M, respectively, as well as the current value of the vector field $\vec{\nu}$. During each iteration, the vector field will change, modifying the correspondences between the static and moving images. Therefore, unlike $\partial\vec{\nu}/\partial P, \partial C/\partial \vec{\nu}$, must be recomputed during each iteration of the optimization problem. Once both terms are computed, they are combined using the chain rule in Eq. (2.8).

Notice that "transforming" the change in the cost function from being in terms of the deformation field to being in terms of the coefficients requires us to employ the B-spline basis functions once again—essentially the reverse operation of what we did when computing the deformation field. Figure 2.4 illustrates the operation of computing the cost function gradient at a single control point (marked in red) for a 2D image. Here, $\partial C/\partial \nu$ has been computed at all voxels including the voxel highlighted in red shown in the zoomed view having local coordinates $(2,1)$ within tile $(0,0)$. The location of this red voxel's tile with respect to the red control point results in the evaluation of the "red piece" of B-spline basis function in both the x and y dimensions. These evaluations are performed using the normalized local coordinates of the voxel; for our red voxel, this would result in evaluating $\beta_0(2/5)$ in

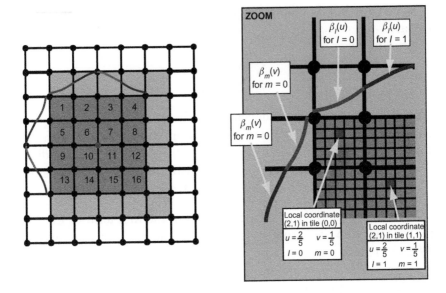

Figure 2.4 A 2D example of parameterizing the cost function gradient using B-splines. Local coordinates are normalized by the number of voxels in the corresponding tile dimensions. This normalization is necessary since the B-spline basis functions are only defined within zero and one.

the x-dimension and $\beta_0(1/5)$ in the y-dimension. These two results and the value of $\partial C/\partial v$ at the voxel in question are multiplied together and the product is stored away for later. Once this procedure is performed at every voxel for each tile in the vicinity of the control point, all of the resulting products are summed together. This results in the value of cost function gradient at the control point in question.

Since this example is in 2D, 16 control points are required to parameterize how the cost function changes at any given voxel with respect to the deformation field. As a result, when computing the value of the cost function gradient at a given control point, the 16 tiles that the control point affects must be included in the computation. These tiles have been highlighted in blue in Figure 2.4. Also, notice how each of the highlighted tiles have been marked with a number between 1 and 16. Each number represents the specific combination of B-spline basis function pieces (red-purple, blue-green, etc.) used to compute a tile's contribution to the cost function gradient at the red control point. In the 2D case, it should be noted that each tile will affect exactly 16 control points and will be subjected to each of the 16 possible B-spline combinations exactly once. This is an important property we exploit when parallelizing this algorithm on the GPU.

On the gradient is calculated, the coefficient values P that minimize the registration cost function are found using L-BFGS-B, a quasi-Newton optimizer suitable for either bounded or unbounded problems (Zhu et al., 1997). During each iteration, the optimizer chooses a set of coefficient values; for these coefficient values, Eqs. (2.1)–(2.6) and Eqs. (2.8)–(2.10) are used to compute the cost and gradient, respectively. The cost and gradient values are transmitted back to the optimizer, and the process is repeated for a set number of iterations or until the cost function converges to a local (or global) minimum.

2.3 B-SPLINE REGISTRATION ON THE GPU

The GPU is an attractive platform to accelerate compute-intensive algorithms such as image registration due to its ability to perform many arithmetic operations in parallel. Our GPU implementations use NVidia's Compute Unified Device Architecture (CUDA), a parallel computing interface accessible to software developers via a set of C programming language extensions. Algorithms written using CUDA can be executed on GPUs such as the Tesla C1060, which consists of 30 streaming multiprocessors (SMs) each containing 8 cores clocked at 1.5 GHz for a total of 240 cores. The CUDA architecture simplifies thread management by logically partitioning threads into equally sized groups called *thread blocks*. Up to eight thread blocks can be scheduled for execution on a single SM. In the context of image registration, a single thread is responsible for processing one voxel, and thus, a thread block is responsible for processing a group of voxels.

This section outlines the overall software organization of our implementations and then describes in depth the GPU kernels that realize the B-spline interpolation and gradient computation steps.

2.3.1 Software Organization

The overall software organization is shown in Figure 2.5 wherein the spline interpolation as well as the cost function and gradient computations are performed on the GPU, while the optimization is performed on the CPU. During each iteration the optimizer, executing on the CPU, chooses a set of coefficient values to evaluate and transmits these to the GPU. The GPU then computes both the cost function and the cost function gradient and returns these to the optimizer. When a minima has been reached in the cost function gradient, the optimizer halts

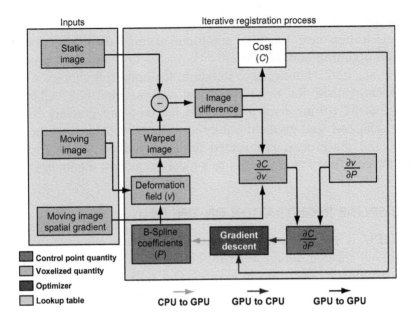

Figure 2.5 Flow chart demonstrating the iterative B-spline registration process. The optimizer alone is executed on the CPU for greater flexibility.

and invokes the interpolation routine on the GPU to compute the final deformation field.

Returning to Figure 2.5, the value of the evaluated cost function C as well as its gradient $\partial C/\partial P$ must be transferred from the CPU to the GPU for every iteration of the registration process. Transfers between the CPU and GPU memories are the most costly in terms of time, and one must take special care to minimize these types of transactions. In our case, the cost function is a single floating point value, and transferring it to the CPU incurs negligible overhead. The gradient, however, consists of three floating point coefficient values for each control point in the grid. For example, registering two $256 \times 256 \times 256$ images with a control grid spacing of $10 \times 10 \times 10$ voxels requires 73,167 B-spline coefficients to be transferred between the GPU and the CPU per iteration, incurring about 0.35 ms over a PCIe 2.0×16 bus. (The PCIe 2.0×16 bus provides a maximum bandwidth of 8 GB/s.) Registering the same two volumes with a control grid spacing of $30 \times 30 \times 30$, $30 incurs 0.30 ms to transfer 5184 coefficients between the GPU and the CPU. Comparable transfer times are incurred in transferring the coefficients generated by the optimizer back to the GPU. Based on detailed profiling experiments on the hardware platform available to us, the CPU-GPU communication overhead demands roughly 0.14% of the total algorithm execution time. We therefore conclude that these PCIe transfers deliver an insignificant impact on the overall algorithm performance even for high-resolution images with fine control grids.

2.3.2 Calculating the Cost Function and $\partial C / \partial \vec{\nu}$

Before the iterative registration process can begin on the GPU, several initialization processes must first be carried out on the CPU in preparation. This consists primarily of initializing the coefficient array P to all zeros, copying data from host memory to GPU memory, and precomputing reusable intermediate values. The *Multiplier LUT* is generated and bound to texture memory for accelerated access on the GPU. Finally, to reduce redundant computations associated with evaluating the cost function, the spatial gradient of the moving image ∇M is computed (not to be confused with the cost function gradient $\partial C / \partial P$). Here, ∇M is a 3D image volume and does not change during the registration process.

The GPU kernel shown in Figure 2.6 calculates the cost function C as well as the $\partial C / \partial \vec{\nu}$ values. It is launched with one thread per voxel in the fixed image S, and the variables (x, y, z) defining the coordinates of a voxel within the volume are derived from each thread's index T_G. As shown in the pseudocode, the coordinates (l, m, n) of the tile housing the voxel of interest as well as the normalized coordinates (u, v, w) of the voxel within the tile are calculated in lines 4 and 7, respectively. Lines 10–17 of the kernel calculate the displacement vectors for the voxel using Eq. (2.1). Lines 23 and 24 apply the deformation vector $\vec{\nu}$ to the moving image to calculate the intensity difference between the fixed image S and moving image M for the voxel in question as well as the SSD cost function C. Finally, lines 27–29 compute $\partial C / \partial \vec{\nu}$ using Eq. (2.10) and store the result to GPU global memory in an interleaved fashion. Calculating C and $\partial C / \partial \vec{\nu}$ exemplifies an algorithm that is easily parallelized on the GPU. Once the kernel has completed, the individual cost function values computed for each voxel are accumulated using a sum reduction kernel to obtain the overall similarity metric C given in Eq. (2.6). Note that to obtain the normalized SSD, we divide the sum by the number of voxels falling within the moving image.

```
 1: /* Get T_G, the 1D index of the thread, and use it to obtain (x, y, z) for the voxel. */
 2:
 3: /* Obtain the coordinates (l, m, n) of the tile within the volume that houses this voxel. */
 4: l = ⌊x/N_x⌋ − 1; m = ⌊y/N_y⌋ − 1; n = ⌊z/N_z⌋ − 1;
 5:
 6: /* Normalized voxel coordinates (x, y, z) to within the range [0, 1]. */
 7: u = x/N_x − ⌊x/N_x⌋; v = y/N_y − ⌊y/N_y⌋; w = z/N_z − ⌊z/N_z⌋;
 8:
 9: /* Use Eq. (2.1) to obtain the displacement vectors for the voxel. */
10: ν_x = ν_y = ν_z = 0;
11: for i = 0 to 3 step 1 do
12:    for j = 0 to 3 step 1 do
13:       for k = 0 to 3 step 1 do
14:          U = β_i(u)β_j(v)β_k(w);
15:          ν_x = ν_x + U × P_x(i + l);
16:          ν_y = ν_y + U × P_y(j + m);
17:          ν_z = ν_z + U × P_z(k + n);
18:       end for
19:    end for
20: end for
21:
22: /* Apply the deformation vector and compute the SSD score for the voxel. */
23: D = S(x, y, z) − M(x + ν_x, y + ν_y, z + ν_z);
24: C(x, y, z) = D²;
25:
26: /* Compute ∂C/∂ν⃗ for the voxel and store to GPU global memory. */
27: ∂C/∂ν[3 × T_G + 0] = 2 × D × ∇M_x(x, y, z);
28: ∂C/∂ν[3 × T_G + 1] = 2 × D × ∇M_y(x, y, z);
29: ∂C/∂ν[3 × T_G + 2] = 2 × D × ∇M_z(x, y, z);
```

Figure 2.6 Code listing for the GPU kernel that calculates the cost function C and $\partial C/\partial\vec{\nu}$.

2.3.3 Calculating the Cost Function Gradient $\partial C/\partial P$

Figure 2.7 outlines our first (and most straightforward) attempt at design-ing a kernel to calculate $\partial C/\partial P$ for a control point as defined by the chain rule in Eq. (2.8) using the $\partial C/\partial\vec{\nu}$ values computed previously by Kernel 1. It is launched with as many threads as there are control points, where each thread computes $\partial C/\partial P$ for its assigned control point. Thus, the operations performed by a single thread to obtain $\partial C/\partial P$ for its con-trol point are done serially, but $\partial C/\partial P$ is calculated in parallel for all con-trol points in the grid. The coordinates of a control point (κ, λ, μ) within the volume are derived from each thread's index T_G. We then identify the 64 tiles influenced by the control point, and for each tile perform the operations detailed in lines 4−27: (i) load the $\partial C/\partial\vec{\nu}$ value for each voxel from GPU memory and calculate the corresponding B-spline basis func-tion product, (ii) compute $\partial C/\partial(\nu) \times \beta_l(u)\beta_m(v)\beta_n(w)$, and (iii) accumu-late the results for each spatial dimension as per the chain rule in Eq. (2.8). Once a thread has accumulated the results for all 64 tiles into

```
 1: /* Use T_G, the 1D thread index, to obtain the (κ, λ, μ) coords of the control point. */
 2:
 3: /* Iterate through the 64 tiles affecting this control point to calculate ∂C/∂P.   Here
    ∂C/∂ν_x(i, j, k) denotes the x-component of the ∂C/∂ν value at voxel (i, j, k) within the tile
    (x_t, y_t, z_t) in the volume, and so on for the y and z components. */
 4: A_x = A_y = A_z = 0;
 5: for l = 0 to 3 step 1 do
 6:   for m = 0 to 3 step 1 do
 7:     for n = 0 to 3 step 1 do
 8:       x_t = κ − n; y_t = λ − m; z_t = μ − l;
 9:
10:       /* For each voxel in tile (x_t, y_t, z_t), compute ∂C/∂P using Eq. (2.8). */
11:       for k = 0 to N_z step 1 do
12:         for j = 0 to N_y step 1 do
13:           for i = 0 to N_x step 1 do
14:             /* Get normalized local voxel coordinates (u, v, w) and compute B-spline basis
                function product. */
15:             U = β_l(u)β_m(v)β_n(w);
16:
17:             /* Accumulate ∂C/∂P values. */
18:             A_x = A_x + U × ∂C/∂ν_x(i, j, k);
19:             A_y = A_y + U × ∂C/∂ν_y(i, j, k);
20:             A_z = A_z + U × ∂C/∂ν_z(i, j, k);
21:           end for
22:         end for
23:       end for
24:
25:     end for
26:   end for
27: end for
28:
29: /* Store the ∂C/∂P solution for the control knot to GPU global memory. */
30: ∂C/∂P[3 ∗ T_G + 0] = A_x;
31: ∂C/∂P[3 ∗ T_G + 1] = A_y;
32: ∂C/∂P[3 ∗ T_G + 2] = A_z;
```

Figure 2.7 Code listing for a straightforward and "naïve" GPU kernel that calculates ∂C/∂P for a control point.

registers $A_x, A_y,$ and $A_z,$ lines 30–32 interleave and insert these values into the $\partial C / \partial P$ array residing in GPU global memory.

Though Kernel 2 details perhaps the most straightforward way of parallelizing $\partial C / \partial P$ calculations on the GPU, it has a very serious performance deficiency in that the threads executing this kernel perform a large number of redundant load operations from GPU global memory. We outline this problem using an example from Figure 2.8. Consider the shaded tile shown in the top-left corner of the volume. The set of voxels within this tile are influenced by a set of 64 control points (of which eight are shown as black spheres). Conversely, voxels within this tile contribute a $\sum \partial C / \partial \vec{\nu} \times \partial \vec{\nu} / \partial P$ value to the gradient calculations of the respective 64 control points as per the chain rule in Eq. (2.8). Now, considering the

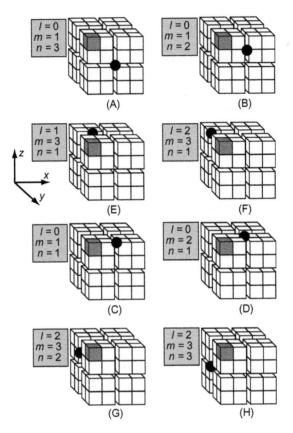

Figure 2.8 Visualization of tile influence on B-spline control points. Voxels within the shaded tile (in the top-left corner of the volume) are influenced by a set of 64 control points, of which eight are shown as black spheres. This tile partially contributes to the gradient values $\partial C/\partial P$ at each of these points. (A)–(H) show that the same tile is utilized in different relative positions with respect to each of the control points influencing it. So, each tile in the volume will be viewed in 64 unique ways by the corresponding 64 control points influencing it, which results in 64 unique (l, m, n) combinations being applied to each tile.

control points shown in Figures 2.8B and C, the position of the tile relative to these two points is $(l = 0, m = 1, n = 2)$ and $(l = 0, m = 1, n = 1)$, respectively. This implies that though the two GPU threads computing the gradient for these control points use the same $\partial C/\partial v$ values belonging to the tile, they must use different basis function products when computing $\partial \vec{v}/\partial P$ to obtain their respective contributions to $\partial C/\partial P$ for the control points they are each working on; the thread responsible for the control point in Figure 2.8B will calculate the contribution of the highlighted tile to $\partial C/\partial P$ as

$$\sum_{N_w} \frac{\partial C}{\partial \vec{v}(x, y, z)} \beta_0(u)\beta_1(v)\beta_2(w)$$

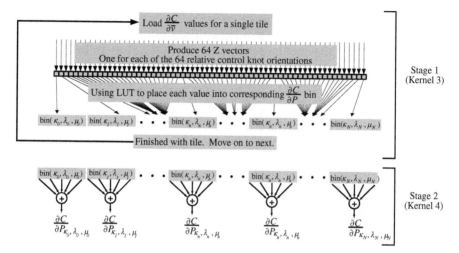

Figure 2.9 The flow corresponding to the "condense" process performed by the optimized GPU implementation. For each tile, we compute all 64 of its $\partial C/\partial P$ contributions to its surrounding control points. These partial contributions are then binned appropriately according to which control points are affected by the tile. We use (κ, λ, μ) to denote the 3D coordinates of a control point within the volume. Notice how each control point is shown as having its own bin that stores all $\vec{Z}$ vectors that contribute to its cost function gradient.

whereas the thread processing the control point in Figure 2.8C will compute the contribution of the highlighted tile to $\partial C/\partial P$ for its control point as

$$\sum_{N_w} \frac{\partial C}{\partial \vec{\nu}(x, y, z)} \beta_0(u)\beta_1(v)\beta_1(w)$$

Here, (u, v, w) represent the normalized position of a voxel within the tile. Since the two threads execute independently of each other and in parallel, each thread will end up loading $\partial C/\partial \nu$ values from the shaded tile separately. In general, given the design of Kernel 2, every tile in the volume will be loaded 64 times by different threads during the process of computing $\partial C/\partial P$ values for the control points. Our goal, therefore, is to develop kernels that eliminate these redundant load operations.

The first step in developing kernels that compute $\partial C/\partial P$ efficiently is to reduce the large amount of $\partial C/\partial \vec{\nu}$ data generated by Kernel 1 residing in GPU global memory into smaller, more manageable chunks. Figure 2.9 shows the overall flow comprising two major stages. During the first stage, the $\partial C/\partial \vec{\nu}$ values corresponding to a tile are read from global memory in coalesced fashion. Since any given voxel tile is influenced by (and influences) 64 control points, it is subject to each of the 64 possible (l, m, n) configurations exactly once. This allows us to form intermediate solutions to Eq. (2.8) as follows, where for each tile, we obtain

$$\vec{Z}_{tile,l,m,n} = \sum_{z=0}^{N_z} \sum_{y=0}^{N_y} \sum_{x=0}^{N_x} \frac{\partial C}{\partial \vec{\nu}(x, y, z)} \beta_l(u)\beta_m(v)\beta_n(w) \qquad (2.11)$$

The above operation is performed for the 64 possible (l, m, n) configurations, resulting in 64 $\vec{Z}$ values per tile, where each $\vec{Z}$ is a partial solution to the gradient computation at a particular control point within the grid. Equation 2.11 can be implemented as a GPU kernel since multiple $\partial C/\partial\vec{\nu}$ tiles may be "condensed" in parallel due to the absence of any data dependencies between tiles. Moreover, once a $\partial C/\partial\vec{\nu}$ tile is read and condensed, it may be discarded since all relevant information required to compute $\partial C/\partial P$ is now represented by the $\vec{Z}$ values. Therefore, the optimized flow shown in Figure 2.9 loads each $\partial C/\partial\vec{\nu}$ value from GPU global memory only once, unlike the design of Kernel 2 where each tile is loaded 64 times by different GPU threads.

Equation 2.11 is applied to each tile in the volume. Once the $\partial C/\partial\vec{\nu}$ values for a tile are condensed into 64 $\vec{Z}$ values, we consult a LUT that maps each $\vec{Z}$ value to one of the 64 control points influenced by the tile. Specifically, the output of this first stage is an array of bins with each bin possessing 64 slots. Each control point in the grid has exactly one bin. For each of the 64 $\vec{Z}$ values computed by Eq. (2.11), the LUT provides not only the mapping to the appropriate control point bin, but also the slot within that bin into which the $\vec{Z}$ value should be stored. Note that each of the 64 $\vec{Z}$ values generated from a single tile will not only be written to different control point bins but to different slots within those bins as well. This property, in combination with each bin of 64 slots starting on an 8-byte boundary, allows us to adhere to the memory coalescence requirements imposed by the CUDA architecture. The second stage of the gradient computation simply sums the 64 $\vec{Z}$ values within each bin to calculate $\partial C/\partial P$ at each control point.

We now discuss the GPU kernels that implement the design flow shown in Figure 2.9. As a first step, Kernel 1 is modified to store $\partial C/\partial\vec{\nu}$ values as three separate noninterleaved arrays whose values can be read in coalesced fashion. Kernel 3, whose pseudocode is shown in Figure 2.10, is designed to be launched with 64 threads operating on a single tile. The outermost loop iterates through the entire set of voxels within the tile in chunks of 64, and during each iteration of this loop, lines 5 and 6 load $\partial C/\partial \vec{v}$ values for the current chunk of voxels into GPU shared memory. Each thread executes lines 14–16 to compute the $\partial C/\partial P$ value contributed by its voxel for the currently chosen basis function product. These values are then accumulated into an array Q, indexed by the (l, m, n) combination, via a tree-style reduction in which all 64 threads contribute (lines 18–25). The inner loops compute the

1: /* Get thread-block index B and the local thead index T. */
2:
3: /* Threads process a $\partial C/\partial \vec{v}$ tile in groups of 64. All threads belonging to a thread block B work on the same tile whose index is denoted by O. This mapping is maintained in a lookup table LUT_{Offset}. */
4: **for** $G = 0$ to $N_w/64$ step 64 **do**
5:      $O = LUT_{\text{Offset}}[B]$;
6:      $\alpha_x[T] = \partial C/\partial v_x[O + G + T]$; $\alpha_y[T] = \partial C/\partial \vec{v}_y[O + G + T]$; $\alpha_z[T] = \partial C/\partial \vec{v}_z[O + G + T]$;
7:
8:      /* Obtain the normalized coordinates (u, v, w) for the voxel within the tile. Code is omitted. */
9:
10:     $P = 0$; // The (l, m, n) combination number, ranging from 0 to 63
11:     **for** $n = 0$ to 3 step 1 **do**
12:        **for** $m = 0$ to 3 step 1 **do**
13:           **for** $l = 0$ to 3 step 1 **do**
14:              $U = \beta_l(u)\beta_m(v)\beta_n(w)$; // Evaluate the basis function product
15:              /* Store the $\partial \vec{C}/\partial P$ value contributed by this voxel. */
16:              $R_x[T] = \vec{\alpha}_x[T] \times U$; $R_y[T] = \vec{\alpha}_y[T] \times U$; $R_z[T] = \vec{\alpha}_z[T] \times U$;
17:
18:              /* Since there are 64 threads operating on different voxels, each thread will generate a $\partial C/\partial P$ value per voxel corresponding to the (l, m, n) combination. Reduce these values to a single value and store in $R_x[0]$, $R_y[0]$, and $R_z[0]$. Code is omitted. */
19:
20:              _syncthreads(); // Threads wait here until the reduction is complete
21:              /* Thread 0 accumulates the $\partial C/\partial P$ values corresponding to this (l, m, n) combination. */
22:              **if** $T = 0$ **then**
23:                 $Q_x[P] = Q_x[P] + R_x[0]$; $Q_y[P] = Q_y[P] + R_y[0]$; $Q_z[P] = Q_z[P] + R_z[0]$;
24:              **end if**
25:              _syncthreads();
26:              $P = P + 1$; // Move on to the next combination
27:           **end for**
28:        **end for**
29:     **end for**
30: **end for**
31: /* Identify the 64 control points affecting the tile using LUT_{CP} and store $\partial C/\partial P$ values to the appropriate bins. */
32: $K = LUT_{\text{CP}}[64 * B + T]$;
33: $V_x[64 \times K + T] = Q_x[T]$; $V_y[64 \times K + T] = Q_y[T]$; $V_z[64 \times K + T] = Q_z[T]$;

Figure 2.10 The first stage of the optimized kernel designed to calculate $\partial C/\partial P$.

next set of $\partial C/\partial P$ values corresponding to a different combination on the same batch of voxels. Once computed, the $\partial C/\partial P$ values are placed into bins corresponding to the control points that influence the tile (lines 31−33). When executed on the NVidia Tesla C1060, approximately 15 tiles can be processed in parallel at any given time.

Kernel 4 implements the second stage of the flow in Figure 2.9. It reduces the 64 $\partial C/\partial P$ values into a final gradient value for each control point. Lines 8−16 use shared memory to interleave the (x, y, z) components of the $\partial C/\partial P$ stream to improve the coalescence of write to GPU global memory in line 18. Kernel 4 is launched with as many threads as there are control points (Figure 2.11).

To summarize, the optimized GPU implementation focuses primarily on restructuring the B-spline algorithm to use available GPU memory and processing resources as effectively as possible. We restructure the data flow of the algorithm so that loads from global memory are performed only once and in a coalesced fashion for optimal bus bandwidth utilization. Data fetched from global memory is placed into shared memory where threads within a thread block may quickly and effectively work together. Furthermore, for efficient parallel processing, we recognize the smallest independent unit of work is a tile. This leads to an interesting situation in which high-resolution control grids provide

```
 1: /* Get the thread index T and the thread-block index B for this thread. */
 2: ξₓ[T] = Vₓ[64 × B + T]; ξ_y[T] = V_y[64 × B + T]; ξ_z[T] = V_z[64 × B + T];
 3: __syncthreads();
 4:
 5: /* Reduce ξ⃗ and store results in ξ⃗[0]. Code is omitted. */
 6:
 7: /* Interleave gradient values in shared memory and store to GPU global memory. */
 8: if T == 0 then
 9:     ψ[0] = ξₓ[0];
10: end if
11: if T == 1 then
12:     ψ[1] = ξ_y[0];
13: end if
14: if T == 2 then
15:     ψ[2] = ξ_z[0];
16: end if
17: if T ≤ 2 then
18:     ∂C/∂P[3 × B + T] = ψ[T];
19: end if
```

Figure 2.11 The second stage of the optimized kernel designed to calculate $\partial C/\partial P$.

many smaller work units while lower resolution ones provide fewer, but larger work units. So, high-resolution grids yield a greater amount of data parallelism than lower resolution ones, leading to better performance on the GPU.

2.4 PERFORMANCE EVALUATION

We present experimental results obtained for the CPU and GPU implementations in terms of both execution speed and registration quality. We compare the performance achieved by six separate implementations: the single-threaded reference code, the multicore OpenMP implementation on the CPU, and four GPU-based implementations. The GPU implementations are the naive method comprising Kernels 1 and 2, and three versions of the optimized implementation comprising of Kernels 1, 3, and 4. The first version uses an LUT of precomputed basis function products, whereas the second version computes these values on the fly. The third version simply implements the standard code optimization technique of loop unrolling in an effort to maximize performance; the innermost loop (lines 13–27) of Kernel 4 is fully unrolled, and the tree style sum reduction portrayed in line 18 is also fully unrolled. The reason for comparing the first two versions of the optimized GPU-based design is to experimentally determine if the GPU can evaluate the B-spline basis functions faster than the time taken to retrieve precomputed values from the relatively slow global memory. We also quantify each implementation's sensitivity to both volume size as well as control point spacing (i.e., the tile size). These tests are performed on a machine with two Intel Xeon E5540 processors (a total of eight CPU cores), each clocked at 2.5 GHz, 24 GB of RAM, and an NVidia Tesla C1060 GPU card. The Tesla GPU contains 240 cores, each clocked at 1.5 GHz and 4 GB of onboard memory. In addition to this comparative performance analysis, we take the best performing algorithm implementations across the single-threaded, multicore, and GPU paradigms and compare their performance using the most modern CPU and GPU platforms available at the time of this writing. For example, the best performing single and multicore CPU algorithms are timed using an Intel i7-3770 CPU with four SMT cores, each clocked at 3.4 GHz, and the best performing GPU algorithm is timed using an NVidia GeForce GTX 680 containing 1536 cores, each clocked at 1.1 GHz, and with 2 GB of onboard memory.

2.4.1 Registration Quality

Figure 2.12 shows the registration of two $512 \times 512 \times 128$ CT images of a patient's thorax on the GPU. The image on the left is the reference image, captured as the patient was fully exhaled, and the image on the right is the moving image, captured after the patient had fully inhaled. The resulting vector field after registration is overlaid on the inhale image. Figure 2.13 is a zoomed-in view of Figure 2.12, focusing

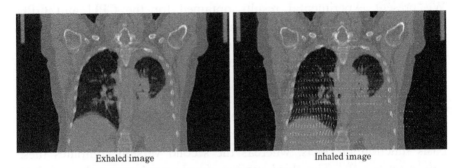

| Exhaled image | Inhaled image |

Figure 2.12 Deformable registration result for two 3D CT images. The deformation vector field is shown superimposed upon inhaled image. The registration is performed using optimized GPU implementation.

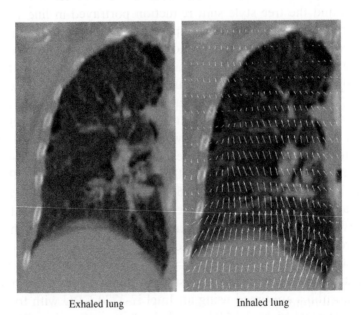

| Exhaled lung | Inhaled lung |

Figure 2.13 An expanded view of the deformable registration result. The superimposed deformation field shows how the inhaled lung has been warped to register to the exhaled lung.

on just the left lung. To determine the registration quality, we generate the deformation field by running the registration process for 50 iterations and then compare the results against the reference implementation. Both the multicore and GPU versions generate near-identical vector fields with an RMS error of less than 0.014 with respect to the reference.

2.4.2 Sensitivity to Volume Size

We test each algorithm's sensitivity to increasing volume size by holding the control point spacing constant at 10 voxels in each physical dimension while increasing the size of synthetically generated input volumes in steps of $10 \times 10 \times 10$ voxels. For each volume size, we record the execution time taken for a single registration iteration to complete. Figure 2.14 shows the results for each of the five implementations. The plot on the left compares all five implementations, where we see that the execution time increases linearly with the number of voxels in a volume. The multicore implementations provide an order of magnitude improvement in execution speed over the reference implementation. For large volume sizes around 350^3 voxels, the most highly optimized GPU implementation achieves a speedup of 15 times compared to the reference code, whereas the multicore CPU implementation achieves a speedup proportional to the number of CPU cores (eight times when executed on dual Xeon E5540 four-core processors). Furthermore, note that the naive GPU implementation cannot handle volumes having more than 4.3×10^7 voxels. Recall that Kernel 2 suffers from a serious performance flaw: redundant and uncoalesced loads of $\partial C/\partial \vec{\nu}$ values from GPU global memory. Using the texture unit as a cache provides a method of mitigation, but the resulting speedup varies unpredictably with control grid resolution (Figure 2.15). Moreover, the texture unit cannot cache very large volumes, limiting the maximum size that the naive implementation can correctly process to about 350^3 voxels.

Finally, Figure 2.15A compares the performance of the serial, OpenMP, and the optimized GPU implementations (LUT, unrolled from Figure 2.14) on the Intel i7-3770 and the GTX 680 GPU for a fixed control point spacing of $20 \times 20 \times 20$ voxels. Figure 2.15B isolates the OpenMP and GPU implementations so that the nature of the performance improvement can better viewed. For these architectures, the

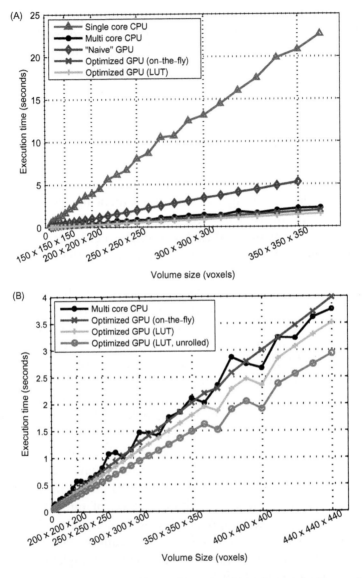

Figure 2.14 (A) The execution time incurred by a single iteration of the registration algorithm as a function of volume size. The control point spacing is fixed at $10 \times 10 \times 10$ voxels. (B) The execution time versus volume size for the various multicore implementations described in the chapter.

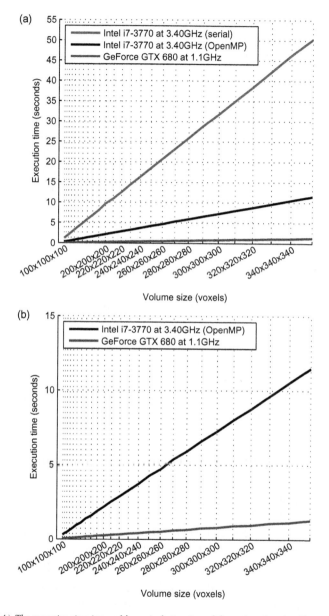

Figure 2.15 (A) The execution time incurred by a single iteration of the registration algorithm as a function of volume size. The control point spacing is fixed at $20 \times 20 \times 20$ voxels. (B) Execution time versus volume size for just the multicore CPU and GPU implementations.

OpenMP implementation outperforms the single-core implementation by a factor of 4.4 times; the GPU implementation outperforms OpenMP by a factor of 8.8 times and the single-core implementation by a factor of 39 times.

2.4.3 Sensitivity to Control Point Spacing

The optimized GPU design achieves short iteration times by assigning individual volume tiles to processing cores as the basic work unit. Since tile size is determined by the spacing between control points, we investigated whether the execution time is sensitive to the control point spacing. Figure 2.16A shows the impact of different grid spacings on our B-spline implementations when the volume size is fixed at $256 \times 256 \times 256$ voxels. Notice that all implementations, except for the naive GPU version, are agnostic to spacing.

Figure 2.16B focuses just on the multicore designs. Interestingly, the multicore CPU implementation outperforms the optimized GPU implementations for coarse control grids, starting at a spacing of about 40 voxels. The higher clocked CPU cores process these significantly larger tiles more rapidly than the lower clocked GPU cores. So, for practitioners doing multiresolution registration, the coarser control grids can be handled by the CPU, whereas the GPU-based design can be invoked as the control point spacing becomes finer.

Figure 2.17A again compares the performance of the serial, OpenMP, and the optimized GPU implementation on the Intel i7-3770 and the GTX 680 for a fixed volume size of $350 \times 350 \times 350$ voxels. As before, Figure 2.17B isolates the OpenMP and GPU implementations so that the nature of the performance improvement can better viewed. Again, it is seen that as the control point spacing increases, the GPU implementation begins to suffer for reasons previously discussed. However, for these newer hardware platforms, the GPU implementation manages to continue to outperform the OpenMP implementation for large work units in spite of the performance bottleneck.

2.5 SUMMARY

This chapter has developed a grid-alignment technique and associated data structures that greatly reduce the complexity of B-spline-based

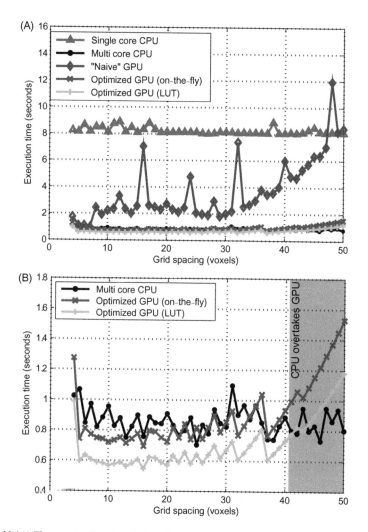

Figure 2.16 (A) The execution time for a single registration iteration is shown as a function of the control point spacing (same in all three dimensions). The volume size is held constant at 256³ voxels. (B) The execution time versus control point spacing for the multicore implementations.

registration. We have then used the main ideas underlying the aligned grid method to develop highly parallel and scalable designs for computing the score and cost function gradient on multicore processors. We have demonstrated the speed and robustness of our parallelization strategy via experiments using both clinical and synthetic data. Our experiments also demonstrate a fairly strong independence between the B-spline grid resolution and execution time for the parallel algorithms.

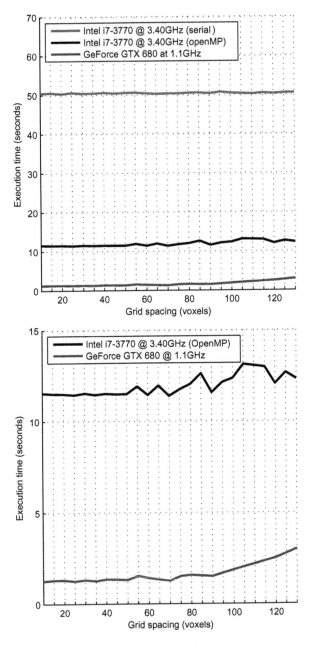

Figure 2.17 (A) The execution time incurred by a single iteration of the registration algorithm as a function of control point spacing. The volume size is fixed at 350 × 350 × 350 voxels. (B) Execution time versus control point spacing for just the multicore CPU and GPU implementations.

REFERENCES

Kybic, J., Unser, M., 2003. Fast parametric elastic image registration. IEEE Trans. Med. Imaging 12 (11), 1427–1442.

Rohlfing, T., Maurer Jr, C.R., 2003. Nonrigid image registration in shared-memory multiprocessor environments with application to brains, breasts, and bees. IEEE Trans. Information Tech. Biomedicine 7 (1), 16–25.

Rohrer, J., Gong, L., Szekely. G., et al., 2008. Parallel mutual information based 3D non-rigid registration on a multi-core platform. MICCAI Workshop High-Performance Medical Image Computing and Computer Aided Intervention, New York, NY, USA.

Rueckert, D., Sonoda, L.I., Hayes, C., Hill, D., Leach, M.O., Hawkes, D.J., 1999. Nonrigid registration using free-form deformations: application to breast MR images. IEEE Trans. Med. Imaging 18 (8), 712–721.

Saxena, V., Rohrer, J., Gong, L., 2010. A parallel GPU algorithm for mutual information based 3D nonrigid image registration. Proc. Int. Euro-Par. Conf. Part II, 223–234.

Shackleford, J., Kandasamy, N., Sharp, G., 2010. On developing B-spline registration algorithms for multi-core processors. Phys. Med. Biol. 55 (21), .6329–6352, Ischia, Italy

Zheng, X., Udupa, J., Chen, X., 2009. Cluster of workstation based nonrigid image registration using free-form deformation. Proceedings of the SPIE 7261, Medical Imaging 2009: Visualization, Image-Guided Procedures, and Modeling, 72611N, Orlando, FL, USA.

Zhu, C., Byrd, R., Nocedal, J., 1997. L-BFGS-B: algorithm 778: L-BFGS-B, FORTRAN routines for large scale bound constrained optimization. ACM Trans. Math. Softw. 23 (4), 550–560.

CHAPTER 3

Multimodal B-Spline Registration

Information in This Chapter
- Overview of Multimodal B-Spline Registration
- Mutual Information as A Cost Function
- Efficient Computation of Mutual Information
- Gradient Descent Optimization to Iteratively Tune the B-Spline Coefficients
- Performance Evaluation

3.1 INTRODUCTION

The B-spline deformable registration algorithm maps each and every voxel in a fixed or static image S to a corresponding voxel in a moving image M as described by a deformation field $\vec{\nu}$, which is defined at each and every voxel within the static image. An optimal deformation field accurately describes how the voxels in M have been displaced with respect to their original positions in S. The existence of such an optimal and physically meaningful deformation field assumes that the two images represent the same underlying physiology. If the images are obtained using the same imaging method, the registration is said to be unimodal and the quality of the deformation field is assessed using the sum of squared differences between the intensity values of voxels in the static image and the corresponding voxels in the warped moving image. Alternatively, images obtained using differing imaging methods must be matched using multimodal registration. The registration modality is important since assessing the quality of the deformation field for multimodal registrations requires more complex methods than those required by unimodal registration. This is due to the involved images having different color spaces which are not guaranteed to possess any type of linear or one-to-one mapping. Mutual information (MI) and normalized MI are widely used similarity metrics when registering multimodality images in which the MI quantifies the amount of information content common to the two images (Thevenaz and Unser, 2000). The images will be optimally aligned when the shared information content is maximized.

High-Performance Deformable Image Registration Algorithms for Manycore Processors.
DOI: http://dx.doi.org/10.1016/B978-0-12-407741-6.00003-7

Figure 3.1 shows the overall process used for registering multimodality images, comprising of the following major steps: (i) generating a deformation field using the B-spline coefficients, (ii) applying the deformation field to the moving image, (iii) generating voxel-intensity histograms for both the static and deformed moving images as well as their joint histogram, (iv) computing the MI using the histograms to assess the registration quality, (v) computing the change in the MI with respect to the B-spline coefficients, and (vi) generating a new set of B-spline coefficients. The above process is repeated until an optimal deformation field is obtained that warps the moving image such that it is most similar to the static image. The number of iterations required depends on factors, such as the severity of the initial misalignment, the complexity of local deformations in the patient's anatomy, and the level of accuracy the end user deems necessary.

Each iteration of the process shown in Figure 3.1 optimizes the deformation field $\vec{v}$, resulting in a more accurate mapping or

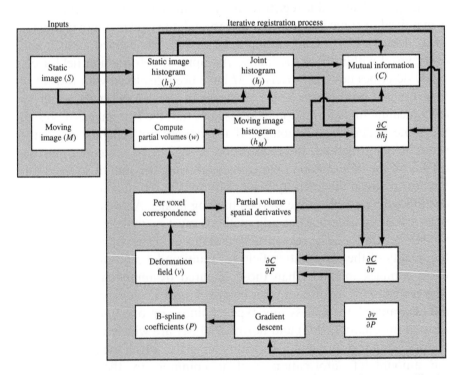

Figure 3.1 The overall process used to register multimodality images using MI as the similarity metric. All major steps in this process (except for the gradient descent optimization) have been parallelized on multi-core processors including the GPU.

correspondence of voxels in the static image to coordinates within the moving image. Any given voxel in the static image can map to a point lying between multiple voxels in the moving image; in 3D images, for example, a voxel in the static image can map to eight neighboring voxels in the moving image. The case of "one-to-many" correspondence is handled via a technique called partial volume interpolation (PVI, Maes et al., 1997) and is discussed in greater detail later in the chapter. Once the correspondence has been performed for a voxel and the partial volumes have been computed, the intensity histograms for the static and moving images, as well as the joint histogram, are updated appropriately. These histograms capture the entropy in the individual images as well as the joint entropy describing the amount of uncertainty when considering both images as a joint system. For 3D images, this means updating one static-image histogram bin, eight moving-image histogram bins, and eight joint-histogram bins. The completed histograms are then used to compute the MI, which measures how similar the static image is to the moving image (after the moving image is subjected to $\vec{\nu}$).

The best registration is obtained by modifying the deformation field $\vec{\nu}$ so as to maximize the MI. This process can be posed as an optimization problem. However, since medical image volumes can be quite large[1] and since the deformation field is defined at every voxel, operating on the vector field directly is a problem too large to handle even for modern computers. For faster computation, the deformation field $\vec{\nu}$ can be parameterized using a sparse number of B-spline coefficients which results in a compressed representation of the deformation field. The problem then becomes one of optimizing the B-spline coefficients $\vec{P}$ to maximize the MI cost function C. Performing this optimization via gradient descent (or quasi-Newtonian) methods requires that we know how the cost function C changes with respect to the B-spline coefficients $\vec{P}$. The steps needed to obtain this derivative $\partial C/\partial P$ are also outlined in Figure 3.2.

3.2 USING B-SPLINES TO REPRESENT THE DEFORMATION FIELD

The material presented in this section has been previously covered in depth in Chapter 2. Here, we provide a recap of the major concepts.

---

[1]A typical image volume has a resolution of $512 \times 512 \times 128$ or about 33 million voxels.

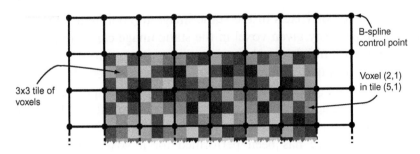

Figure 3.2 The code listing for a kernel that obtains the deformation vector at a given voxel.

Given a number of uniformly spaced discrete control points, a second-order continuous function involving these points can be described using uniform cubic B-spline basis functions. Describing a function in this fashion is advantageous when the desired function is unknown but we are required to maximize an optimization condition while maintaining second-order continuity. In deformable image registration, the deformation field $\vec{\nu}$ that maps voxels in the static image to voxels in the moving image must maintain this level of smoothness; yet the form of $\vec{\nu}$ is not known when starting the registration process since $\vec{\nu}$ depends on the geometry of the anatomy being registered. It is therefore advantageous to parameterize the dense deformation field $\vec{\nu}$ using a sparse set of control points which are uniformly distributed throughout the fixed image's voxel grid. The placement of control points forms two grids that are aligned to one another: a dense voxel grid and a sparse control-point grid. As shown in Figure 3.3, the control-point grid partitions the voxel grid into equally sized regions called tiles. The deformation field $\vec{\nu}$ can be found at any given voxel within a tile by performing B-spline interpolation using control points with local support regions that include the tile. Since the local support region for a cubic spline curve involves four control points in each of the three dimensions, computing a single point in the displacement field involves the 64 control points found in the immediate vicinity of a voxel's housing tile. Also, since three coefficients p_x, p_y, and p_z are associated with each control point, the interpolation uses 192 coefficients.

Mathematically, the x component of the deformation field for a voxel located at coordinates $\vec{x} = (x, y, z)$ in the fixed image can be described as

```
1: function decompress_vector ($\vec{c}$, $\vec{N}$, $\vec{p}$, $\vec{q}$)
2:    /* vector $\vec{c}$ contains the control-point grid dimensions */
3:    /* vector $\vec{N}$ contains the tile dimensions */
4:    /* vector $\vec{p}$ contains the voxel's tile coordinates */
5:    /* vector $\vec{q}$ contains the voxel's local coordinates within the tile */
6:    /* Returns $\vec{\nu}$, the displacement vector at voxel */
7:
8:    $\vec{\nu} = 0.0$
9:    for $k = 0$ to 3 step 1 do
10:       $n = p_z + k$
11:       $\beta_n = \text{LUT\_Bspline\_z}[k \times N_z + q_z]$
12:       for $j = 0$ to 3 step 1 do
13:          $m = p_y + j$
14:          $\beta_m = \text{LUT\_Bspline\_y}[j \times N_y + q_y]$
15:          for $i = 0$ to 3 step 1 do
16:             $l = p_x + i$
17:             $\beta_l = \text{LUT\_Bspline\_x}[i \times N_x + q_x]$
18:
19:             /* Get index into coefficient look up table clut, given $l, m, n$ */
20:             $\text{cidx} = 3 \times ((n \times c_x \times c_y) + (m \times c_x) + l)$
21:
22:             /* Add the control point's contribution to displacement vector */
23:             $Q = \beta_l \times \beta_m \times \beta_n$
24:             $\nu_x = \nu_x + Q \times \text{clut}[\text{cidx} + 0]$
25:             $\nu_y = \nu_y + Q \times \text{clut}[\text{cidx} + 1]$
26:             $\nu_z = \nu_z + Q \times \text{clut}[\text{cidx} + 2]$
27:          end for
28:       end for
29:    end for
30:    return $\vec{\nu}$
31: end function
```

Figure 3.3 The grid of uniformly spaced B-spline control points partitions the voxel grid into equally sized tiles. In this example, each tile is three voxels wide and three voxels tall. The number of control points in the x dimension is three greater than the number of tiles in the x dimension. Although not shown, this is true for all dimensions.

$$\nu_x(\vec{x}) = \sum_{i=0}^{3} \sum_{j=0}^{3} \sum_{k=0}^{3} \beta_i(u)\beta_j(v)\beta_k(w)p_x(l, m, n) \qquad (3.1)$$

The components in the y and z directions are defined similarly. The symbols l, m, and n are indices for control points in the neighborhood of the tile of interest, and in the 3D case there are 64 combinations for l, m, and n. If (N_x, N_y, N_z) are the dimensions, in voxels, of a tile, then $\lfloor x/N_x \rfloor - 1$, $\lfloor y/N_y \rfloor - 1$, and $\lfloor z/N_z \rfloor - 1$ denote the x, y, and z coordinates, respectively, of the tile in the volume within which a voxel $\vec{\nu}$ falls, and the set of control points indexed by l, m, and n is

$$l = \left\lfloor \frac{x}{N_x} - 1 + i \right\rfloor, \quad m = \left\lfloor \frac{y}{N_y} - 1 + j \right\rfloor, \quad n = \left\lfloor \frac{z}{N_z} - 1 + k \right\rfloor \qquad (3.2)$$

In Eq. (3.1), β_i is the B-spline basis function along the x direction given as

$$\beta_i(u) = \begin{cases} \dfrac{(1-u)^3}{6} & i = 0 \\[2ex] \dfrac{3u^3 - 6u^2 + 4}{6} & i = 1 \\[2ex] \dfrac{-3u^3 + 3u^2 + 3u + 1}{6} & i = 2 \\[2ex] \dfrac{u^3}{6} & i = 3 \end{cases} \qquad (3.3)$$

with β_j and β_k defined similarly in the y and z directions, respectively. Finally, $\vec{q} = (u, v, w)$ denotes the local coordinates of voxel $\vec{x}$ within its housing tile where

$$u = \frac{x}{N_x} - \left\lfloor \frac{x}{N_x} \right\rfloor, \quad v = \frac{y}{N_y} - \left\lfloor \frac{y}{N_y} \right\rfloor, \quad w = \frac{z}{N_z} - \left\lfloor \frac{z}{N_z} \right\rfloor \qquad (3.4)$$

Since the basis function is only defined within the range between 0 and 1, the local coordinates are appropriately normalized to fall within this range.

Representing the dense deformation field as a sparse set of B-spline coefficients is akin to information compression and the deformation field is optimized by modifying only its compressed form. In other words, the deformation field is never directly modified but is always tuned via the B-spline coefficient values. Obtaining the deformation field from B-spline coefficients is akin to a decompression operation, which is needed to check the registration quality. Figure 3.2 shows the process of obtaining a deformation vector at a single voxel. The vector's coordinate, $\vec{x}$, is specified in terms of the coordinate pair $(\vec{p}, \vec{q})$. The tile $\vec{p}$ within which the deformation vector is computed determines the set of 64 B-spline control points involved in the decompression operation. The local coordinate $\vec{q}$ is used to retrieve the precomputed evaluation of the B-spline basis function stored within the lookup tables LUT_Bspline_x, LUT_Bspline_y, and LUT_Bspline_z. Line 20 uses the control-point indices (l, m, n) and the dimensions of the control-point grid to compute a one-dimensional

Organization of coefficient look-up table:

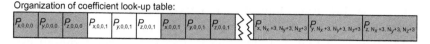

Figure 3.4 Organization and memory layout of the coefficient lookup table. The number of control points in the control grid is greater than the number of tiles by three in each dimension as shown in Figure. 3.2.

index into the data structure used to store the B-spline coefficients (Figure 3.4). Finally, lines 23−26 accumulate the contribution of control point (l, m, n) to the three components of $\vec{\nu}(\vec{x})$.

Obtaining the entire deformation field is a simple matter of applying the technique shown in Figure 3.2 for every voxel $\vec{x}$ in the static image S. The most effective single instruction, multiple data (SIMD)-style threading model on the GPU to obtain the correspondence between the static and moving images is to assign one thread per voxel S. Given an execution grid of threads, each thread uses its unique identifier within the grid to locate the voxel and compute the voxel's tile and local coordinates, $\vec{p}$ and $\vec{q}$, respectively. Once these coordinates are obtained, each thread can decompress the vector at its voxel location in parallel using the operations listed in Figure 3.2. Once a thread has obtained the deformation vector $\vec{\nu}$, it continues to work independently to find the correspondence in the moving image, which will consist of a group of eight voxels. The thread then computes the partial volumes associated with this neighborhood of voxels and accumulates them into the image histograms. The lookup tables LUT_Bspline_x, LUT_Bspline_y, LUT_Bspline_z, and clut are stored as textures to accelerate memory reads through the caching provided by the GPU's texture unit.

3.3 MI AS A COST FUNCTION

A cost function or similarity metric is used to determine the quality of the deformation field $\vec{\nu}$, which is equivalent to assessing the registration quality since $\vec{\nu}$ directly determines the voxel correspondence between the static and moving images. The cost function for assessing the quality of a unimodal registration simply accumulates the square of the intensity difference between the static image S and the moving image M subject to the deformation field $\vec{\nu}$ as

$$\frac{1}{N}\sum_{z}\sum_{y}\sum_{x}(S(x, y, z) - M(x + \nu_x, y + \nu_y, z + \nu_z))^2 \qquad (3.5)$$

where N is the total number of voxels mapping from S to M. However, this cost function cannot be used to assess the quality of a deformation field that is attempting to register images acquired using different imaging modalities since these images may have differing voxel-intensity maps for identical anatomy. For such multimodality registrations, the more sophisticated cost function of MI may be used which qualifies the amount of information content the two images share in common; the images will be optimally aligned when the shared information content is maximum. To understand MI as a cost function, consider the intensity a of a voxel located at coordinates $\vec{x}$ within the static image, $a = S(\vec{x})$, and the intensity b of a voxel at coordinates $\vec{y}$ within the moving image, $b = M(\vec{y})$. The goal is to apply a coordinate transform $T(\vec{y})$ to the moving image such that it registers best with the static image. The statistical MI is obtained as

$$I = \sum_{a,b} p_j(a, T(b)) \ln \frac{p_j(a, T(b))}{p_S(a) p_M(T(b))} \tag{3.6}$$

which depends on the probability distributions of the voxel intensities in the static and moving images. So, we can view a and b as random variables with associated probability distribution functions $p_S(a)$ and $p_M(b)$, respectively, and joint probability $p_j(a, b)$. Applying the spatial transformation $T(\vec{y})$ to M modifies $p_j(a, b)$ and this effect is implied using the notation $p_j(a, T(b))$. Furthermore, if T results in voxels being displaced outside of the moving image, $p_M(T(b))$ will change, and if T results in a voxel being remapped to a location that falls between points on the voxel grid, some form of interpolation must be employed to obtain b, which will modify $p_M(b)$ as well. These effects are implied using the notation $p_M(T(b))$.

The interpolation method used to obtain b, given $T(\vec{y})$, is important both in terms of executions speed and convergence time. Our implementation uses the PVI method (Maes et al., 1997). Figure 3.5A shows an example of computing partial volumes for 2D images in which the deformation vector has mapped a pixel to the static image to a point falling within a neighborhood of four pixels in the moving image. The pixel centers are shown as black circles and the interpolation point is denoted by Δ. The interpolation method divides the volume defined by the four neighboring pixels into corresponding partial

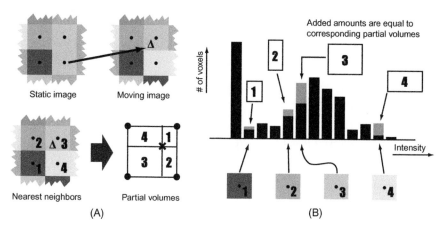

Figure 3.5 (A) PVI for 2D images using a neighborhood of four voxels. Notice that the first partial volume is the smallest since the first neighbor is the furthest away from the interpolation point Δ. *(B) The nearest neighbor voxels are binned according to their intensity values. The amount added to each bin is determined by each voxel's corresponding partial volume which is equivalent to adding fractional voxels to each histogram bin involved in the interpolation operation.*

volumes that share the interpolation point in common. Once the partial volumes are computed, they are placed into the histogram bins of the corresponding voxels as shown in Figure 3.5B.

For 3D images, PVI is performed using a neighborhood of eight voxels where the partial volumes w_0-w_7 are defined in terms of the interpolation point Δ as shown by the `compute_pv()` function in Figure 3.6. Note that $\sum_{i=0}^{7} w_i = 1$. Once the partial volumes have been computed, they are placed into the histogram bins of the corresponding voxels: partial volume w_0 is placed into the histogram bin associated with the neighboring voxel n_0, w_1 with n_1, and so on. The indices of the bins are computed using the `find_nearest_neighbors()` function, also listed in Figure 3.6. The PVI technique is used to compute both $p_M(T(b))$ and $p_j(a, T(b))$. Since the static image is not subject to the coordinate transform **T**, PVI does not apply when generating $p_S(a)$. However, if **T** results in a voxel $\vec{x}$ within S mapping outside of M, then that voxel is not included in the distribution $p_S(a)$. Such voxels cannot be registered, and so are excluded when computing the cost function and related items like intensity distributions.

Given that the coordinate transformation **T** is defined by the deformation field $\vec{\nu}$ such that $T(b) = M(T(\vec{y})) = M(\vec{x} + \vec{\nu}) = M(\vec{\Delta})$, an

```
 1: /* Compute partial volumes */
 2: function compute_pv (Δ⃗)
 3: /* Here { } is the sawtooth function (i.e.  {x} = x − ⌊x⌋) */
 4:    w₀ = (1 − {Δₓ}) × (1 − {Δ_y}) × (1 − {Δ_z})
 5:    w₁ = (0 + {Δₓ}) × (1 − {Δ_y}) × (1 − {Δ_z})
 6:    w₂ = (1 − {Δₓ}) × (0 + {Δ_y}) × (1 − {Δ_z})
 7:    w₃ = (0 + {Δₓ}) × (0 + {Δ_y}) × (1 − {Δ_z})
 8:    w₄ = (1 − {Δₓ}) × (1 − {Δ_y}) × (0 + {Δ_z})
 9:    w₅ = (0 + {Δₓ}) × (1 − {Δ_y}) × (0 + {Δ_z})
10:    w₆ = (1 − {Δₓ}) × (0 + {Δ_y}) × (0 + {Δ_z})
11:    w₇ = (0 + {Δₓ}) × (0 + {Δ_y}) × (0 + {Δ_z})
12:    return w⃗
13: end function
14:
15: /* Computes indices of the eight nearest neighbors */
16: function find_nearest_neighbors (Δ⃗, M_X, M_Y)
17: /* M_X and M_Y are the dimensions of the moving image in the x and y
    directions, respectively */
18:    n₀ = (⌊Δ_z⌋ × M_X × M_Y) + (⌊Δ_x⌋ × M_X) + ⌊Δ_x⌋
19:    n₁ = n₀ + 1
20:    n₂ = n₀ + M_X
21:    n₃ = n₂ + 1
22:    n₄ = n₀ + M_X × M_Y
23:    n₅ = n₄ + 1
24:    n₆ = n₄ + M_X
25:    n₇ = n₆ + 1
26:    return n⃗
27: end function
```

Figure 3.6 Computation of the partial volumes as well as the nearest neighbors.

algorithm to compute the MI cost function C is best implemented by modifying Eq. (3.6) as

$$C = \frac{1}{N} \sum_{j=0}^{K_S} \sum_{i=0}^{K_M} h_j(i,j) \ln \frac{N \times h_j(i,j)}{h_S(j) \times h_M(i)} \tag{3.7}$$

where the probability distributions $p_S(a)$, $p_M(T(b))$, and $p_j(a, T(b))$ are constructed as image histograms h_S, h_M, and h_j consisting of K_S, K_M, and $K_S \times K_M$ bins, respectively. Also, Eq. (3.7) incorporates N, the number of voxels being registered, thereby allowing the use of unnormalized histograms (which reduces the number of division operations during histogram generation).

3.4 EFFICIENT COMPUTATION OF MI

Evaluating the MI-based cost function in Eq. (3.7) requires constructing the image histograms h_S, h_M, and h_j. Generating these histograms using a

```
 1: /* Calculate the appropriate bin in the static-image histogram and increment it
    */
 2: /*    h_S[ ] is an array containing histogram values */
 3: /*    B_S is the destination bin for voxel a = S(x⃗) */
 4: /*    O_S is the minimum static-image voxel value */
 5: /*    D_S is the histogram bin spacing */
 6: B_S = ⌊(S(x⃗) − O_S)/D_S⌋
 7: h_S[B_S] = h_S[B_S] + 1
 8:
 9: /* Use the deformation vector v⃗ to find nearest neighbors and partial volumes
    */
10: n⃗ = find_nearest_neighbors (x⃗ + v⃗, M_X, M_Y)
11: w⃗ = compute_pv (x⃗ + v⃗)
12:
13: /* Add partial volumes to the moving-image histogram and the joint histogram */

14: /*    h_M[ ] is an array containing the moving-image histogram values */
15: /*    h_J[ ] is a 2D array of values in the joint histogram */
16: /*    B_M is the destination bin for voxel b = S(n⃗_x)*/
17: /*    O_M is the minimum moving-image voxel value */
18: /*    D_M is the histogram bin spacing */
19: for i = 0 to 7 step 1 do
20:     B_M = ⌊(M(n_i) − O_M)/D_M⌋
21:     h_M[B_M] = h_M[B_M] + w_i
22:     h_j[B_M][B_S] = h_j[B_M][B_S] + w_i
23: end for
```

Figure 3.7 A serial method of histogram construction. (The expanded definitions of the functions find_nearest_neighbors() *and* compute_pv() *can be found in Figure 3.6.)*

serial (or single-threaded) program, as shown in Figure 3.7, is straightforward. First, the voxel $a = S(\vec{x})$ found at the tail of the deformation vector located at $\vec{x}$ is processed for inclusion in the static-image histogram $h_S(a)$. This is a simple matter of determining which bin the intensity value a falls within and incrementing it by one (lines 6 and 7). The second operation is to compute the coordinates of the eight corresponding voxels, $n_0 - n_7$, associated with $T(\vec{y})$ within the moving image by looking at the head of the deformation vector $\vec{v}$ with the tail placed at $\vec{x}$ (line 10). Similarly, the partial volumes, $w_0 - w_7$, are obtained in line 11 for PVI.

For each of the eight voxels, the associated bin within the moving-image histogram h_M is incremented by the corresponding partial volume (lines 20 and 21). Additionally, the joint-histogram bins of interest are easily found using the appropriate bin within h_S and the eight bins within h_M. Each of these bins within the joint histogram h_j is incremented by the appropriate partial volume (line 22). After the process outlined in Figure 3.7 is performed for every voxel in that static image processing a correspondence, the image histograms are complete—keeping in mind that voxels mapping to coordinates outside the moving image have no correspondence.

The algorithm listed in Figure 3.7 is invoked for each vector $\vec{\nu}$ in the deformation field and since the number of vectors equals the number of voxels found in the static image, this algorithm must be invoked N times. When trying to improve computational efficiency, the algorithm cannot simply be invoked in parallel across N threads due to write hazards associated with histogram construction wherein two or more threads attempt to increment the same histogram bin simultaneously. We use two separate thread-safe techniques: one targeting h_S and h_M and the other targeting h_j to construct the image histograms in parallel on the GPU. Since both methods make effective use of the memory hierarchy available within the GPU, we familiarize the reader with this topic via the following brief discussion. The interested reader is referred to Kirk and Hwu (2012) for more details.

The memory hierarchy within a GPU is comprised of registers, shared memory, and global memory. Registers provide the fastest access but are also the most scarce in number. They exhibit thread-level scope, meaning every thread is assigned a set of registers that store data that is private to that thread. Shared memory is the fastest memory type accessible to multiple threads; it exhibits what is known as thread-block scope. Since GPU kernels can comprise of thousands of threads, these threads are grouped into many smaller sets called thread blocks of up to 512 threads each, and each thread block is assigned a modest amount of shared memory that allows the threads within the block to communicate quickly with each other. The size of the shared memory assigned to a thread block ranges from 16 KB to 48 KB on various GPU platforms. Finally, ranging on the order of gigabytes, global memory is the largest yet slowest memory available. It is accessible to every thread, which provides a means for thread blocks to communicate with each other. Furthermore, global memory is how the CPU and GPU exchange data and it remains persistent between multiple kernel invocations. Consequently, kernels generally begin with a read from global memory and end with a write to global memory.

3.4.1 Constructing Histograms for the Static and Moving Images

This technique partitions an image into many nonoverlapping subregions. Each subregion is assigned to a unique thread block which then generates a histogram for its assigned subregion of the image, where the size of a subregion (in voxels) equals the number of threads within a thread block. Figure 3.8 describes the operations performed by a thread block computing the moving-image histogram, beginning with each thread obtaining the deformation vector $\vec{\nu}$ corresponding to its assigned voxel $\vec{x}$ within the subregion delegated to the thread block. Given $\vec{\nu}$, each thread computes the eight nearest neighbors in the moving image corresponding to its assigned voxel $\vec{x}$ and the weights associated with each of these neighbors by computing the partial volumes (lines 4 and 5). Upon reaching line 8, each thread has local copies of 16 items: the indices of the nearest neighbors and the associated weights. At this point, all threads simultaneously place each of the

```
 1: /* Note:  Each thread is assigned a deformation vector ν⃗ */
 2:
 3: /* Each thread finds nearest neighbors and partial volumes */
 4: n⃗ = find_nearest_neighbors (x⃗ + ν⃗, M_X, M_Y)
 5: w⃗ = compute_pv (x⃗ + ν⃗)
 6:
 7: /* Accumulate weights into shared memory array s_partitions */
 8: /* Here threadIdx is the index of the thread within the thread block */
 9: for i = 0 to 7 step 1 do
10:     B_M = ⌊(M(n_i) - O_M)/D_M⌋
11:     idx = threadIdx + B_M × threadsPerBlock
12:     s_partitions[idx] = s_partitions[idx] + w_i
13: end for
14:
15: /* Synchronize threads to this point */
16: __syncthreads()
17:
18: /* Assign each thread to a single sub-histogram bin */
19: if threadIdx < num_bins then
20:     sum = 0.0
21:     element = (threadIdx) AND (0x0F)
22:     offset = threadIdx × threadsPerBlock
23:
24:     /* Merge bin partitions */
25:     for i = 0 to (threadsPerBlock - 1) step 1 do
26:         sum = sum + s_partitions[offset + element]
27:         element = element + 1
28:         if element = threadsPerBlock then
29:             element = 0
30:         end if
31:     end for
32:     /* Each bin has now been merged */
33:
34:     /* Write merged bins to sub-histogram for this thread block */
35:     /* Here, blockIdxInGrid denotes the index of a thread block within the grid
           of thread blocks */
36:     sub_hist[blockIdxInGrid * num_bins + threadIdx] = sum
37: end if
```

Figure 3.8 A parallel method of histogram construction using sub-histograms.

Organization of s_partitions[ ]:

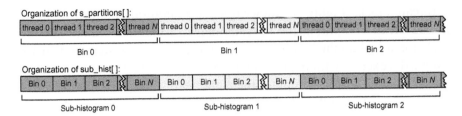

Organization of sub_hist[ ]:

Figure 3.9 Memory organization for the sub-histogram method showing the graphical representation of the memory layout for arrays s_partition[ ] and sub_hist[ ] used in Figure 3.8.

eight weights into the moving-image histogram bins associated with the intensity values of the nearest neighbors (lines 9–13).

Since all threads within a thread block perform the operations listed in Figure 3.8 concurrently, we must ensure that threads wishing to modify the same histogram bin do not modify the same memory location simultaneously. If a thread block has N_B threads, we divide each bin into N_B partitions as shown in Figure 3.9. This data structure, s_partitions, resides within the GPU's shared memory and allows each thread to have its own copy of each histogram bin, which prevents write collisions. On line 16, all threads within the thread block are synchronized to ensure that each has incremented its personal copy of the moving-image histogram before moving on to the next step of merging the partitions within each bin. This operation, shown in lines 19–36, assigns one thread to each bin. Because the number of partitions equals the number of threads within the thread block, each thread merging a partition performs N_B accumulation operations to complete the process. All bins can be processed in parallel in this fashion since there are no dependencies between bins. However, some special considerations must be taken due to the way shared memory is organized. Shared memory is organized as 16 banks of 1 KB memory each. If two threads attempt to read from the same memory bank simultaneously, the reads become serialized, which negatively impacts performance. We therefore aim to minimize these bank conflicts by starting each thread off on a different bank as shown in line 21. Thread 0 sums its N_B partitions starting with partition 0, residing in the first bank; thread 1 starts with partition 1, residing in the second bank, sums through to N_B and then "wraps around" to end on partition 0, and so on. This way, each thread responsible for merging the partitions within a bin in s_partitions will always read from a different shared-memory bank when generating a histogram with up to 16 bins. For histograms with more than 16 bins, bank conflicts will occur when reading, but they will be minimal; to construct an 18-bin histogram, for example, threads 0 and 16 will read bank 1 simultaneously, and threads 1 and 17 will read bank 2 simultaneously, while the reads issued by threads 2–15 will remain free of conflicts.

Once each thread has merged the partitions of a bin down to a single value (lines 25–31), the threads copy the histogram bins to the sub_hist array residing in the GPU's global memory (line 36), where thread block 0 writes out the sub-histogram 0, thread block 1 writes out sub-histogram 1, and so on. Once all thread blocks have written their sub-histograms to sub_hist, a simple tree-style sum reduction kernel is used to merge these sub-histograms into one histogram that is representative of the moving image M.

3.4.2 Constructing the Joint Histogram

The above-described method cannot be used to generate the joint histogram h_j since GPUs typically do not have sufficient shared memory to maintain individual copies of the joint histogram for each thread within a thread block. Therefore, the proposed method, detailed in Figure 3.10, relies on atomic operations available in more recent GPU models to guarantee mutually exclusive access to histogram bins and requires considerably less shared memory.

For popular older GPU modules (such as the Tesla C1060 and the GTX 200 series Nvidia GPUs), atomic addition operations on floating-point values residing in global or shared memories are not supported. However, these models support atomic-exchange operations on floating-point values residing in shared memory; one can safely swap a value in a shared-memory location with a register value that is private to the thread. The technique discussed below uses the concept of atomic exchange to regulate access to histogram bins and avoid write conflicts between multiple threads. More recent GPUs can simply replace lines 16–24 with an atomic addition instruction.

The image is once again divided into subregions, each of which is assigned to individual thread blocks to generate the corresponding sub-histograms. However, instead of maintaining a separate partition for each thread within a bin, all threads write to the same bin in shared memory. So, for a joint histogram with $K_J = K_S \times K_M$ bins, K_J elements of shared memory are allocated per thread block. This array, s_joint, holds the entire sub-histogram for the thread block. Write conflicts to

```
 1: /* Note:   Each thread is assigned a deformation vector v⃗ */
 2:
 3: /* Each thread finds nearest neighbors and partial volumes */
 4: n⃗ = find_nearest_neighbors (x⃗ + v⃗, M_X, M_Y)
 5: w⃗ = compute_pv (x⃗ + v⃗)
 6:
 7: /* Compute the fixed histogram bin and joint offset */
 8: B_S = ⌊(S(x⃗) − O_S)/D_S⌋
 9: offset = B_S × K_M
10:
11: /* Add partial volumes to joint histogram */
12: for i = 0 to 7 step 1 do
13:     B_M = ⌊(M(n_i) − O_M)/D_M⌋
14:     idx = offset + B_M
15:     if idx != inferred_bin then
16:        success = FALSE
17:        while success == FALSE do
18:           val =atomicExch(s_joint[idx], −1)
19:           if val! = −1 then
20:              success = TRUE
21:              val = val + w_i
22:              atomicExch(s_joint[idx], val)
23:           end if
24:        end while
25:     end if
26: end for
27:
28: /* Copy sub-histogram from shared to global memory */
29: chunks = (K_J × block_size − 1) ÷ block_size
30: for i = 0 to chunks step 1 do
31:     idx = threadIdx + i × block_size
32:     if idx < K_J then
33:        j_hist[j_stride + idx] = s_joint[idx]
34:     end if
35: end for
```

Figure 3.10 Parallel histogram construction using the atomic-exchange operation.

the same bin are handled using the atomic-exchange instruction, as shown in lines 16–24. The GPU instruction atomicExch(x, y) allows a thread to swap a value x in a shared-memory location with a register value y that is private to the thread, while returning the previous value of x. If multiple threads attempt to exchange their private values with the same memory location simultaneously, it is guaranteed that only one will succeed. Returning to line 18, the successful thread obtains a private copy of the histogram value in `val`, leaves the value -1 in the shared-memory locations `s_joint[ idx]`, and proceeds to lines 20–23; other threads attempting to access the same bin simultaneously will obtain the -1 previously placed into shared memory. This technique, therefore, provides an efficient mechanism of serializing threads attempting to write to the same memory location simultaneously. Note that the threads proceeding to line 20 increment the histogram value `val` obtained from shared memory by the appropriate partial volume weight (line 21), exchange the incremented value back into shared memory (thus removing the -1 placed earlier), and set their `success` flag to `TRUE` to indicate that their contributions to the joint histogram have been committed. Finally, lines 29–35 copy the sub-histogram from shared memory to the GPU's global memory.

When generating the joint histogram, we also perform a simple but key optimization step to improve computational efficiency. Since medical images generally contain a predominant intensity—for example, black, which is the intensity value of air, is abundant in most CT scans—the technique presented here can result in the serialization of many threads if they all update histogram bins involving this value. We prevent this situation, however, by inferring the value of the bin corresponding to the predominant value since this bin is expected to cause the most write conflicts. Since the sum of all unnormalized histogram bins must equal the total number of voxels in the static image having a correspondence within the moving image, one bin may be omitted during the histogram construction phase and filled in later using the simple relationship

$$h_j(\text{inferred\_bin}) = N - \sum_i h_j(i) \qquad (3.8)$$

where `inferred_bin` is the bin that is skipped in line 15 of Figure 3.10. Initially, an educated guess is made for `inferred_bin` based on the imaging modality, but as the registration is performed over multiple iterations, the largest bin is tracked and skipped for the next iteration. Experimental results using CT images indicate a noticeable speedup, since on average, 80% of GPU threads attempt to bin values correlating to air which would otherwise be serialized.

3.4.3 Evaluating the Cost Function
Once the histograms are generated, evaluating the MI-based cost function is straightforward, consisting of simply cycling through these

histograms while accumulating the results of the computation into C as in Eq. (3.7). Care must be taken, however, to avoid evaluating the natural logarithm of zero in instances where the joint-histogram bin is empty. Since the operation does not substantially benefit from parallelization, it is performed on the CPU. Moving the histogram data from the GPU to the CPU requires negligible time since even large histograms incur very small transfer times on a modern PCIe bus. Once evaluated, a single cost value is copied back to the GPU for use in subsequent operations.

3.4.4 Optimizing the B-Spline Coefficients

Since we have chosen the coordinate transformation $T(\vec{y}) = \vec{x} + \vec{v}$, where $\vec{v}$ is parameterized in terms of the sparse B-spline coefficients $\vec{P}$, it follows that the MI can be maximized by optimizing these coefficients. We choose to perform this optimization of gradient descent for which an analytic expression for the gradient $\partial C / \partial \vec{P}$ is required at every control point $\vec{P}$. The expression $\partial C / \partial \vec{P}$ can be separated into partial derivatives using the chain rule:

$$\frac{\partial C}{\partial \vec{P}} = \frac{\partial C}{\partial \vec{v}} \times \frac{\partial \vec{v}}{\partial \vec{P}} \tag{3.9}$$

where the first term depends on the similarity metric. The second term depends on the parameterization of the deformation field $\vec{v}$ and is easily obtained by taking the derivative of Eq. (3.1) with respect to $\vec{P}$ as

$$\frac{\partial \vec{v}}{\partial \vec{P}} = \sum_{l=0}^{3} \sum_{m=0}^{3} \sum_{n=0}^{3} \beta_l(u)\beta_m(v)\beta_n(w) \tag{3.10}$$

In the first term of Eq. (3.9), C and $\vec{v}$ are coupled through the probability distribution p_j and are therefore directly affected by the PVI. This becomes clearer when $\partial C / \partial \vec{v}$ is further decomposed as

$$\frac{\partial C}{\partial \vec{v}} = \frac{\partial C}{\partial p_j(a, M(\vec{\Delta}))} \times \frac{\partial p_j(a, M(\vec{\Delta}))}{\partial \vec{v}}$$

$$= \sum_{x=0}^{7} \left(\frac{\partial C}{\partial p_j(a, M(n_x))} \times \frac{\partial w_x}{\partial \vec{v}} \right) \tag{3.11}$$

where $M(\vec{\Delta})$ is the value of the voxel in the moving image that corresponds to the static-image voxel $a = S(\vec{x})$. However, since $\vec{\Delta}$ falls between voxels in the moving image, eight moving-image voxels of varying weights are taken to correspond to $\vec{x}$ due to the PVI, resulting in the simplification as shown in Eq. (3.11). The first term of Eq. (3.11) is obtained using the derivative of Eq. (3.6) with respect to the joint distribution p_j as

$$\frac{\partial C}{\partial p_j(a, M(n_x))} = \ln \frac{p_j(a, M(n_x))}{p_S(a)p_M(M(n_x))} - C \qquad (3.12)$$

The second term describes how the joint distribution changes with the vector field. Recall that the displacement vector locally transforms the coordinates of a voxel in the moving image M such that $\vec{\Delta} = \vec{x} + \vec{\nu}$. As the vector field is modified, the partial volumes, $w_0 - w_7$, are to be inserted into the moving-image and joint histograms h_M and h_j will change in size. Therefore, $\partial p_j(a, M(\vec{\Delta}))/\partial\vec{\nu}$ is determined by changes exhibited in the partial volumes $w_0 - w_7$ as $\vec{\Delta}$ evolves with the governing deformation field $\vec{\nu}$. These changes in the partial volumes with respect to the deformation field $\partial w_x/\partial\vec{\nu}$ for $x \in [0, 7]$, with respect to each of the Cartesian directions are easily obtained, thus resulting in 24 expressions. (The mathematical expressions for $w_0 - w_7$ can be found in the compute_pv() function as shown in Figure 3.6). So, for partial volume w_0:

$$\frac{\partial w_0}{\partial \nu_x} = (-1) \times (1 - \{\Delta_y\}) \times 1 - \{\Delta_z\} \qquad (3.13)$$

$$\frac{\partial w_0}{\partial \nu_y} = (-1) \times (1 - \{\wedge_x\}) \times 1 - \{\Delta_z\} \qquad (3.14)$$

$$\frac{\partial w_0}{\partial \nu_z} = (-1) \times (1 - \{\Delta_x\}) \times 1 - \{\Delta_y\} \qquad (3.15)$$

and similarly for $w_1 - w_7$. Therefore, as prescribed by Eq. (3.11), computing $\partial C/\partial\nu$ at a given voxel $\vec{x}$ in S involves cycling through the eight bins corresponding to the neighbors described by $\vec{\Delta}$. So, for the first neighbor n_0, we determine which bin B_{M_0} within histogram h_M the voxel value n_0 belongs. This gives $h_M(B_{M_0})$. Similarly, the bin B_S within the static-image histogram h_S associated with the static-image voxel $a = S(\vec{x})$ is easily obtained, thus giving $h_S(B_S)$. Knowing B_S and B_{M_0} gives the associated joint-histogram value $h_j(B_S, B_{M_0})$. Now, $\partial C/\partial p_j$ for neighbor n_1 is obtained as

$$\frac{\partial C}{\partial p_j(a, M(n_0))} = \ln \frac{h_j(B_S, B_{M_0})}{h_S(B_S)h_M(B_{M_0})} - C \qquad (3.16)$$

As prescribed by Eq. (3.11), the contribution of nearest neighbor n_0 and its associated partial volume w_0 on $\partial C/\partial \vec{\nu}$ is found by first computing $\partial w_0/\partial \vec{x}$ as in Eq. (3.15). Each of the three components of $\partial w_0/\partial \vec{x}$ are weighted by Eq. (3.16), leading to

$$\frac{\partial C}{\partial \nu_x} = \left(\frac{\partial w_0}{\nu_x} \times \frac{\partial C}{\partial p_j}\Big|_{n_0}\right) + \left(\frac{\partial w_1}{\nu_x} \times \frac{\partial C}{\partial p_j}\Big|_{n_1}\right) + \cdots \qquad (3.17)$$

$$\frac{\partial C}{\partial \nu_y} = \left(\frac{\partial w_0}{\nu_y} \times \frac{\partial C}{\partial p_j}\Big|_{n_0}\right) + \left(\frac{\partial w_1}{\nu_y} \times \frac{\partial C}{\partial p_j}\Big|_{n_1}\right) + \cdots \qquad (3.18)$$

$$\frac{\partial C}{\partial \nu_z} = \left(\frac{\partial w_0}{\nu_z} \times \frac{\partial C}{\partial p_j}\Big|_{n_0}\right) + \left(\frac{\partial w_1}{\nu_z} \times \frac{\partial C}{\partial p_j}\Big|_{n_1}\right) + \cdots \qquad (3.19)$$

which gives $\partial C/\partial \vec{\nu}$ at the static-image voxel coordinate $\vec{x}$. This operation is performed for all N voxels in S.

The operations needed to compute $\partial C/\partial \vec{\nu}$ are performed in parallel by assigning a GPU thread to each voxel in the static image that has a correspondence in the moving image. Figure 3.11 shows the operations performed by each thread. Once $\partial C/\partial \vec{\nu}$ has been computed at every voxel, we can now use Eq. (3.9) to describe how the cost function changes with the B-spline coefficients $\vec{P}$ associated with each control

```
 1: n⃗ = find_nearest_neighbors (Δ⃗, M_X, M_Y)
 2:
 3: /* Compute partial volumes spatial derivatives */
 4: ∂w⃗/∂x = compute_pv_derivatives_x (Δ⃗)
 5: ∂w⃗/∂y = compute_pv_derivatives_y (Δ⃗)
 6: ∂w⃗/∂z = compute_pv_derivatives_z (Δ⃗)
 7:
 8: /* Calculate static image histogram bin */
 9: B_S = ⌊(S(x⃗) − O_S)/D_S⌋
10:
11: /* Compute ∂C/∂ν⃗ at voxel coordinate x⃗ */
12: for i = 0 to 7 step 1 do
13:     B_M = ⌊(M(n_i) − O_M)/D_M⌋
14:     ∂C/∂p_j = ln((N × h_j[B_M][B_S])/(h_S[B_S] × h_M[B_M])) − C
15:     ∂C/∂ν_x = ∂C/∂ν_x + ∂w_i/∂x × ∂C/∂p_j
16:     ∂C/∂ν_y = ∂C/∂ν_y + ∂w_i/∂y × ∂C/∂p_j
17:     ∂C/∂ν_z = ∂C/∂ν_z + ∂w_i/∂z × ∂C/∂p_j
18: end for
```

Figure 3.11 Computing the derivative of the cost function with respect to vector field.

point. Figure 3.12 shows an example of how the cost-function gradient is obtained at a single control point, highlighted in white, in a 2D image. Here, $\partial C / \partial \vec{\nu}$ has been computed at all voxels, including the hatched voxel shown in the zoomed-in view at local coordinates $(1,1)$ within tile $(0,0)$. The locations of this hatched voxel's tile with respect to the highlighted control point result in the evaluation of the B-spline basis function with $l = 0$ and $m = 0$ in the x and y dimensions, respectively. Moreover, these evaluations are performed using the normalized coordinates of the voxel within the tile, therefore evaluating $\beta_0(1/3)$ and $\beta_0(1/3)$ in the x and y dimensions, respectively. These two results and the value of $\partial C / \partial \vec{\nu}$ at the voxel in question are multiplied together and the product is stored away for later. Once this procedure is performed at every voxel for each tile in the vicinity of the control point, all of the resulting products are accumulated, resulting in the value of the cost-function gradient $\partial C / \partial \vec{P}$ at the control point.

Since the example in Figure 3.12 uses a 2D image, 16 control points are needed to parameterize how the cost function changes at any given voxel with respect to the deformation field. Therefore, when computing the value of the cost-function gradient at a given control point, the 16 tiles affected by the control point must be included in the computation; these tiles are numbered $1-16$ in the figure. Each tile number represents a specific combination of the B-spline basis-function pieces used to compute a

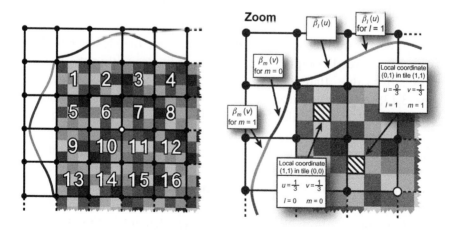

Figure 3.12 A 2D example of the cost-function gradient computation. The process of re-expressing $\partial C / \partial \vec{\nu}$ in terms of the B-spline control point coefficients yields the cost-function gradient $\partial C / \partial \vec{P}$ at each control point. This is partially demonstrated for the control point highlighted in white.

tile's contribution to the gradient at the highlighted control point. For example, voxels within tile number 1 use basis functions with $l = 0$ and $m = 0$ in the x and y directions, respectively; voxels within tile 2 use basis function with $l = 1$ and $m = 0$, and so on. Furthermore, in the 2D case, each tile of $\partial C/\partial \vec{\nu}$ affects exactly 16 control points and is therefore subjected to each of the 16 possible B-spline combinations exactly 1. In the 3D case, each tile affects 64 control points. This is an important property that forms the basis of our parallel implementation of this algorithm.

The GPU-based algorithm computes $\partial C/\partial \vec{P}$ operations on tiles instead of individual voxels. Here, one thread block of 64 threads is assigned to each tile in the static image. Given a tile in which $\partial C/\partial \vec{\nu}$ values are defined at each voxel location, the 64 threads work together to parameterize these derivative values in terms of the B-spline control-point coefficients, namely a sec of $\partial C/\partial \vec{P}$ values. Since 64 control points are needed to parameterize a tile's contents using cubic B-splines, the thread block will contribute to the gradient values defined at the 64 control points in the tile's immediate vicinity. In fact, each control point in the grid will receive such gradient value contributions from exactly 64 tiles (or thread blocks). The final value of the cost-function gradient at a given control point is the sum of the 64 contributions received from its surrounding tiles.

Figure 3.13 shows the multistage process of computing the x component of $\partial C/\partial \vec{P}$ in parallel on the GPU. This process takes as input, the starting address of the tile within the $\partial C/\partial \vec{\nu}$ array that is associated with the thread block. During stage 1, the 64 threads work in unison to fetch a cluster of 64 contiguous $\partial C/\partial \vec{\nu}$ values from global memory, which are then stored into register. Once the cluster has been loaded, each thread computed the local coordinates within the tile for the $\partial C/\partial \vec{\nu}$ value that it is responsible for. Also, as shown in Figure 3.13, the input values are zero padded to 64, which was chosen to make the tile size a multiple of thread-block size. The padding prevents a cluster from reading into the next tile when the control-point configuration results in tiles that are not naturally a multiple of the cluster size. Stage 2 sequentially cycles through each of the 64 possible B-spline piece was function combinations, using the local coordinates of the $\partial C/\partial \vec{\nu}$ values previously computed in Stage 1. Each of the 64 function combinations are applied to each element in the cluster in parallel; the results are stored in a temporary array located within the GPU's shared memory which is then reduced to a single value and

Stage1 -- Each thread loads a value from the current cluster

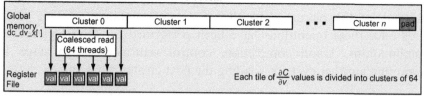

Stage 2 -- Each thread calculates all 64 possible B-spline basis function products for its dC_dv value

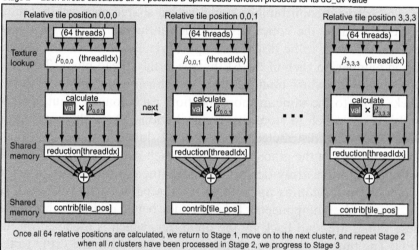

Stage 3 -- Sort condensed tile's contributions to approtriate control point bins in preparation for final sum reductions

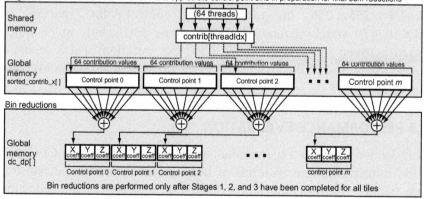

Figure 3.13 The gradient computation workflow showing the process of computing the cost-function gradient $\partial C/\partial \vec{P}$ in parallel. Computation of the x component of $\partial C/\partial \vec{P}$ is depicted. Components in the y and z directions are calculated similarly.

accumulated into `sorted_contrib_x`, a region of shared memory indexed by the piecewise B-spline function combination. This stage ends once these operations have been performed for the 64 piecewise combinations. Upon completion, control returns back to stage 1, beginning another cycle by loading the next cluster of 64 values.

Once stage 2 has processed all the clusters within a tile, we will have 64 gradient contributions stored within shared memory that must be distributed to the control points they influence. Stage 3 assigned one contribution, to be distributed appropriately based on the combination number, to each of the 64 threads in the thread block. To avoid race conditions when multiple threads belonging to different thread blocks write to the same memory location, each control point is given 64 "slots" in which to store these contributions. Once all contribution values have been distributed, each set of 64 slots is reduced to a single value, resulting in the gradient $\partial C/\partial \vec{P}$ at each control point. As shown in Figure 3.13, the array `dc_dp` that holds the gradient is organized in a interleaved fashion as opposed to using separate arrays for each of the x, y, and z components. This provides better cache locality when these values are read back by the optimizer, which is executed on the CPU. The time needed to copy the `dc_dp` array from the GPU to the CPU over the PCIe bus is negligible; for example, registering two $256 \times 256 \times 256$ images with a control-point spacing of $10 \times 10 \times 10$ voxels requires 73,167 B-spline coefficients to be transferred between the GPU and the CPU per iteration, which incurs a transfer overhead of 0.35 ms over a PCIe 2.0×16 bus.

3.5 PERFORMANCE EVALUATION

This section presents experimental results obtained for the CPU and GPU implementations in terms of both execution speed and registration quality. We compare the performance achieved by the following different implementations:

- *Single-threaded CPU implementation.* This reference implementation serves as a baseline for comparing the performance of the multi-core CPU and GPU implementations. It is highly optimized and uses the Streaming SIMD Extensions (SSE) instruction set to acceleration pointing point operations when applicable. Characterizing its performance using Valgrind, a profiling system for Linux programs

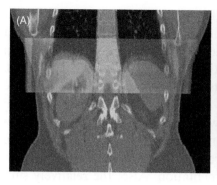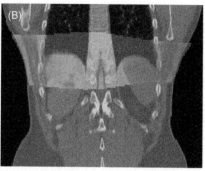

Figure 3.14 Thoracic MRI to CT registration using MI. (A) A $512 \times 384 \times 16$ *voxel MRI volume (shown in red) is superimposed on a* $512 \times 512 \times 115$ *voxel CT volume (shown in blue) prior to deformable registration. (B) The same MRI and CT volumes superimposed on each other after 20 iterations of the deformable registration process on the GPU. The control-point grid spacing is set to* 100^3 *voxels. (For interpretation of the references to color in this figure legend, the reader is referred to the web version of this book.)*

(Nethercote and Seward, 2007), indicates a very low miss rate of about 0.1% in both the L1 and L2 data caches.

- *Multi-core implementation on the CPU using OpenMP.* This implementation uses OpenMP, a portable programming interface for shared-memory parallel computers (Chapman et al., 2007), to parallelize the steps involving histogram generation, cost-function evaluation, and gradient computation.
- *GPU-based implementation.* This implementation uses the compute unified device architecture or CUDA programming interface to perform both histogram generation and gradient computation on the GPU. The cost-function evaluation and the gradient descent optimization are performed on the CPU.

In addition to the registration quality, we quantify the impact of the volume size and control-point spacing on the execution times incurred by each of the above implementations. The tests reported here use a machine equipped with a quad-core Intel i7-3770 processor with Simultaneous multithreading (SMT) in which each core is clocked at 3.4 GHz. The GPU used is the NVidia GeForce GTX 680 model with 1536 cores, each clocked at 1.1 GHz, and with 2 GB of on-board memory. This GPU is a compute capability 3.0 CUDA device (Figure 3.14).

3.5.1 Registration Quality

This series of tests characterizes each implementation's sensitivity, in terms of execution time, to increasing volume size where the volumes are synthetically generated. We fix the control-point spacing at 20 voxels in each physical dimension and increase the volume size in steps of $10 \times 10 \times 10$ voxels. For each volume size, we record the execution time incurred by a single iteration of the registration process. Figure 3.15A summarizes the results. As expected, the execution time increases linearly with the number of voxels involved. The OpenMP versions offers better performance with respect to the reference implementation, with a speedup of 4.4 times. The GPU achieves a speedup of 28 times with respect to the reference implementation and 6.3 times with respect to the OpenMP implementation. Also, the relatively simple optimization step of inferring the value of the histogram bin expected to incur the most write conflicts (in other words, the most number of atomic operations) significantly improves performance on the GeForce GTX 680 GPU; for actual CT data, this optimization step speeds up the histogram generation phase by five times. Finally, the `atomicAdd()` instruction available on newer models like the GeForce GTX 680 allows bins to be incremented in a thread-safe manner without having to perform the complex atomic-exchange logic shown in lines 15–25 of the histogram generation algorithm listed in Figure 3.10.

3.5.2 Sensitivity to Control-Point Spacing

As discussed earlier, the parallel gradient computation exploits key attributes of the uniform control-point spacing scheme to achieve fast execution times. We consider each tile in the volume as a work unit where each unit is farmed out to individual cores that are single threaded in the case of a CPU core or multi-threaded in the case of a GPU. If the volume size is fixed, then increasing the control-point spacing results in fewer, yet larger, work units. Figure 3.15B shows the impact of varying the control-point spacing in increments of $5 \times 5 \times 5$ voxels with the volume size fixed at $350 \times 350 \times 350$ voxels. Note that the execution times are relatively unaffected by the control-point spacing for all implementations.

The GPU-based versions show a slight sublinear increase in execution time starting at a control-point spacing of approximately 65 voxels. For larger spacings, the work-unit size becomes adequately large such that the processing time dominates the time required to swap work units in and out. When the time needed to process a work unit is significantly less than the overhead associated with swapping it in and

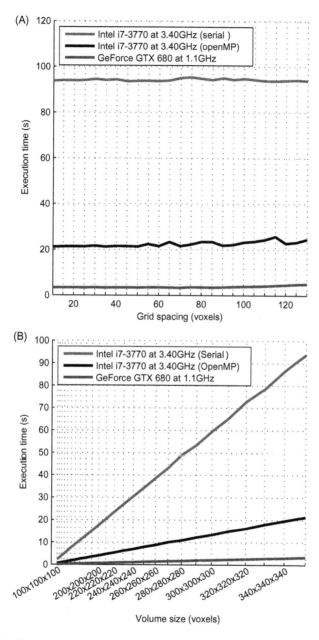

Figure 3.15 (A) The impact of volume size on the execution times incurred by the single-threaded and multi-threaded CPU implementations and the GPU implementations. The control-point spacing is fixed at $20 \times 20 \times 20$ voxels. (B) The impact of control-point spacing on the execution times incurred by the single-threaded and multi-threaded CPU implementations and the GPU implementations. The volume size is fixed at $350 \times 350 \times 350$ voxels.

out of a GPU core, the execution time is essentially constant since the overhead incurred by the swapping is constant. When the processing time begins to dominate, we expect the execution time to increase as the number of elements within the work unit increases.

3.6 RELATED WORK

Other researchers have attacked the problem of multimodal registration using GPUs as well and this section provides the reader with an overview of some existing work, focusing on the following specific areas: B-spline interpolation and histogram generation. The B-spline interpolation step generates the deformation field and some existing techniques aim to accelerate this step using GPUs (Modat et al., 2010; Ruijters et al., 2008; Sigg and Hadwiger, 2005). The B-spline interpolation method described by Ruijters et al. (2008) uses the GPU's linear interpolation hardware as originally proposed by Sigg and Hadwiger (2005). The arguments for this method are based on the reduction of memory reads required to interpolate a single point (from 64 to 8 in the 3D case) and the ability of the GPU's interpolation unit to deliver these 8 interpolated reads faster than it can provide the 64 noninterpolated reads. Naturally, the quality of the interpolation depends on the arithmetic precision supported by the underlying texture hardware. In our work, we use the floating-point units on the GPU to compute the deformation field and use 32-bit floating-point representation throughout to improve the accuracy of the registration process.

Shams et al. consider the rigid registration of multimodality images using MI and focus on accelerating the histogram generation step on the GPU (Shams et al., 2010). The authors apply a concept termed "sort and count" to compute histogram bins in a collision-free manner, thereby eliminating the need for atomic operations. The basic idea uses a parallel version of bitonic sort to order the array of input elements while simultaneously counting the number of occurrences of each unique element in the sorted set; the outcome of the sort returns a single non-zero counter value for each unique value in the input set. Multiple threads can, in parallel, use these counters to update the histogram bins corresponding to each unique element in the input set. The authors present performance results for this technique using input sets comprising of unsigned integers. Comparing the above-described method to our methods of histogram generation, the major difference is that our techniques are specifically aimed at generating histograms with floating-point bin values. Floating-point representation is necessary to correctly handle the case of one-to-many voxel correspondence wherein a voxel in the static-image maps to a point lying between multiple neighboring voxels in the moving image. This situation is handled via a technique called PVI which requires adding fractional voxels, i.e., floating-point values, to histogram bins. A comparison-based sorting strategy like bitonic sort will be computationally expensive since the cost of comparing floating-point numbers is significantly higher than that of comparing integers. Theoretically, any algorithm that can sort integers can be used to sort floating-point values by converting the float into an integer representation that achieves the same sorted order as the float and then translating back to the floating-point format. However, the conversion to a comparable integer format will be exceedingly difficult, if not impossible, in the context of our application. Therefore, one needs to develop histogram generation methods that use atomic intrinsics supported by the underlying instruction set architecture of more recent GPU models while mitigating the impact of thread serialization.

Shams and Kennedy develop a histogram generation method in which the input image is partitioned into many nonoverlapping subregions and each subregion is assigned to a thread block that generates a histogram for its assigned subregion; these individual histograms are then merged into one histogram (Shams and Kennedy, 2007). This method was developed before the availability of GPU platforms supporting atomic intrinsics and as a result, uses software-based synchronization mechanisms to regulate access to the histogram bins; software-based synchronization solutions incur much higher overhead than atomic intrinsics.

3.7 SUMMARY

We have developed a B-spline based deformable registration process for aligning multimodality images, suitable for use on multi-core processors and GPUs. Using MI as the similarity metric, the goal is to obtain a deformation field that warps the moving image such that it is most similar to the static image. We developed and implemented parallel algorithms to realize the following major steps of the registration process: generating a deformation field using the B-spline control-point grid, calculating the image histograms needed to compute the MI, and calculating the change in the MI with respect to the B-spline coefficients for the gradient descent optimizer. We have evaluated the multicore CPU and GPU implementations in terms of both execution speed and registration quality. Our results indicate that the speedup varies with volume size and the voxel-intensity distribution within the images, but is relatively insensitive to the control-point spacing. Our GPU-based implementations achieve, on average, a speedup of 28 times with respect to the reference implementation and 6.3 times with respect to a multi-core CPU implementation using four cores, with near-identical registration quality.

REFERENCES

Chapman, B., Jost, G., Pas, R.V.D., 2007. *Using OpenMP: Portable Shared Memory Parallel Programming*. MIT Press, Cambridge, MA, USA.

Kirk, D., Hwu, W.-M., 2012. Programming Massively Parallel Processors: A Hands-on Approach, second ed. Morgan Kaufmann, Waltham, MA, USA.

Maes, F., Collignon, A., Vandermeulen, D., Marchal, G., Seutens, P., 1997. Multimodality image registration by maximization of mutual information. IEEE Trans. Med. Imaging 16 (2), 187–198.

Modat, M., et al., 2010. Fast free form deformation using graphics processing units. Comput. Methods Programs Biomed. 98 (3), 278–284.

Nethercote, N., Seward, J., 2007. Valgrind: a framework for heavyweight dynamic binary instrumentation. In: ACM SIGPLAN Conference on Programming Language Design Implementation, San Diego, CA, USA, pp. 89–100.

Ruijters, D., Haar-Romeny, B., Suetens, P., 2008. Accuracy of GPU-based B-spline evaluation. IASTED International Conference Computer Graphics Imaging. Acta Press, Innsbruck, Austria, pp. 117–122.

Shams, R., Kennedy, R., 2007. Efficient histogram algorithms for Nvidia CUDA compatible devices. In: International Conference on Signal Processing and Communications Systems, Gold Coast, Australia, pp. 418–422.

Shams, R., Sadeghi, P., Kennedy, R., Hartley, R., 2010. Parallel computation of mutual information on the GPU with application to real-time registration of 3D medical images. Comput. Methods Programs Biomed. 99 (2), 133–146.

Sigg, C., Hadwiger, M., 2005. Fast third-order texture filtering. *GPU Gems* 2. Morgan Kaufmann, Waltham, MA, USA, pp. 313–329.

Thevenaz, P., Unser, M., 2000. Optimization of mutual information for multi-resolution image registration. IEEE Trans. Image Process. 9 (12), 2083–2099.

CHAPTER 4

Analytic Vector Field Regularization for B-spline Parameterized Methods

Information in This Chapter:
- Theory and Mathematical Formalism behind Analytical Regularization
- Algorithmic Implementation
- Performance Evaluation and Sensitivity Analysis

4.1 INTRODUCTION

B-spline-based deformable registration has become a popular method for deriving coordinate system transforms between image volumes exhibiting complex local variations due to its compact local support, rapid computation, and applicability to both single and multimodalities. Such transforms allow nonrigid structures to be mapped between images and provide a quantitative measure of local motion and volumetric change over time. However, due to the inherent ill-posed nature of image registration, the existence of a unique mapping is not guaranteed and the solution space must, therefore, be confined to only physically meaningful transforms. To this end, several regularization methods have been proposed: Rueckert et al. (1999) propose penalizing high thin-plate bending energy whereas Rohlfing et al. (2003) penalize local deviations from a unity Jacobian determinate. Miller et al. (1993) propose minimizing linear elastic energy. Li et al. (2009) enforce a maximum delta between adjacent B-spline coefficients, whereas Chun and Fessler propose encouraging invertible diffeomorphic transforms by placing more complex constraints upon coefficients. In this chapter, we build upon (Rueckert et al., 1999) by developing and validating a fast analytic method for computing the thin-plate bending energy penalty via a set of static matrix operators.

4.2 THEORY AND MATHEMATICAL FORMALISM

Given a uniformly spaced control-point grid as shown in Figure 4.1, the bending energy of the entire deformation may be expressed as a

High-Performance Deformable Image Registration Algorithms for Manycore Processors.
DOI: http://dx.doi.org/10.1016/B978-0-12-407741-6.00004-9

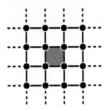

Figure 4.1 A 2-D region supported by 16 control points.

linear combination of the bending energies computed within the individual regions of the B-spline control grid. Therefore, the goal of the approach is to develop an operator that computes the bending energy within a region as a function of the B-spline control points that support the region.

Given a three-dimensional fixed image F with voxel coordinates $\vec{\theta} = x, y, z$ and voxel intensity $f = F(\vec{\theta})$ and moving image M with voxel coordinates $\phi = x_2, y_2, z_2$ and voxel intensity $m = M(\phi)$ representing the same underlying anatomy as F within the image overlap domain Ω, the two images F and M are said to be registered when the cost-function

$$C = \sum_{\vec{T}(\vec{\theta}) \in \vec{\Omega}} \Psi(f, m) + \lambda S \tag{4.1}$$

is optimized according to the similarity metric Ψ under the coordinate mapping $\vec{T}(\vec{\theta}) = \theta + \nu$. Here $\vec{\nu}$ is the dense vector field defined for every voxel $\vec{\theta} \in \Omega$, which is assumed to be capable of providing a good one-to-one mapping from F to M. The smoothness S of $\vec{\nu}$ is added to C with weight λ to drive $\vec{T}$ to a physically meaningful coordinate map. When represented sparsely via the uniform cubic B-spline basis, the vector field $\vec{\nu}$ is parameterized by the set of B-spline basis coefficients $\vec{P}_{i,j,k} = \vec{p}_x, \vec{p}_y, \vec{p}_z$ where

$$\vec{p}_x = \begin{bmatrix} p_{x,0,0,0} \\ \vdots \\ p_{x,I,J,K} \end{bmatrix}, \quad \vec{p}_y = \begin{bmatrix} p_{y,0,0,0} \\ \vdots \\ p_{y,I,J,K} \end{bmatrix}, \quad \vec{p}_z = \begin{bmatrix} p_{z,0,0,0} \\ \vdots \\ p_{z,I,J,K} \end{bmatrix} \tag{4.2}$$

are defined for $n = I \times J \times K$ control points with real-world spacing $\vec{r} = r_x, r_y, r_z$. From this new basis, the vector field may be expressed at a point $\vec{\theta}$ with Euclidean coefficients $\vec{\nu}$ computed via the following tensor product using the 64 B-spline coefficients supporting $\vec{\theta}$:

$$\nu_x = \sum_{i=0}^{3}\sum_{j=0}^{3}\sum_{k=0}^{3}\vec{P}_{i,j,k}\sum_{a=0}^{3}Q_x^{(\delta_x)}(i,a)\vec{x}(a)\sum_{b=0}^{3}Q_y^{(\delta_y)}(i,b)\vec{y}(b)\sum_{c=0}^{3}Q_z^{(\delta_z)}(i,c)\vec{z}(c)$$

(4.3)

for the x-dimension and similarly for the y- and z-dimensions. Here

$$\vec{x} = [1 \; x \; x^2 \; x^3]^T \tag{4.4}$$

forms a Cartesian basis and $\vec{y}$ and $\vec{z}$ are defined similarly. The matrices $Q_x^{(\delta)}$, $Q_y^{(\delta)}$, are $Q_z^{(\delta)}$ are defined by

$$Q_x^{(\delta)} = BR_x\Delta^{(\delta)}, \quad Q_y^{(\delta)} = BR_y\Delta^{(\delta)}, \quad Q_z^{(\delta)} = BR_z\Delta^{(\delta)} \tag{4.5}$$

where B forms the cubic B-spline basis and R_x, R_y, and R_z confine the evaluation of the B-spline basis to $\in [0, 1]$:

$$B = \frac{1}{6}\begin{bmatrix} 1 & -3 & 3 & 1 \\ 4 & 0 & -6 & 3 \\ 1 & 3 & 3 & -3 \\ 0 & 0 & 0 & 0 \end{bmatrix}, \quad R_x = \begin{bmatrix} 1 & 0 & 0 & 0 \\ 0 & \dfrac{1}{r_x} & 0 & 0 \\ 0 & 0 & \dfrac{1}{r_x^2} & 0 \\ 0 & 0 & 0 & \dfrac{1}{r_x^3} \end{bmatrix} \tag{4.6}$$

The matrix $\Delta^{(\delta)}$ is defined for $\delta \in [0, 2]$ as follows:

$$\Delta^{(0)} = \begin{bmatrix} 1 & 0 & 0 & 0 \\ 0 & 1 & 0 & 0 \\ 0 & 0 & 1 & 0 \\ 0 & 0 & 0 & 1 \end{bmatrix}, \quad \Delta^{(1)} = \begin{bmatrix} 0 & 0 & 0 & 0 \\ 1 & 0 & 0 & 0 \\ 0 & 2 & 0 & 0 \\ 0 & 0 & 3 & 0 \end{bmatrix},$$

$$\Delta^{(2)} = \begin{bmatrix} 0 & 0 & 0 & 0 \\ 0 & 0 & 0 & 0 \\ 2 & 0 & 0 & 0 \\ 0 & 6 & 0 & 0 \end{bmatrix}$$

(4.7)

and provides a convenient method for obtaining ν' and ν'' with respect to the Euclidean basis as required by the calculation of the smoothness penalty (Rueckert et al., 1999):

$$
S = \int_{\Omega} \left(\frac{\partial^2 \vec{\nu}}{\partial x^2} \right)^2 + \left(\frac{\partial^2 \vec{\nu}}{\partial y^2} \right)^2 + \left(\frac{\partial^2 \vec{\nu}}{\partial z^2} \right)^2 + \left(\frac{\partial^2 \vec{\nu}}{\partial xy} \right)^2
$$
$$
+ \left(\frac{\partial^2 \vec{\nu}}{\partial xz} \right)^2 + \left(\frac{\partial^2 \vec{\nu}}{\partial yz} \right)^2 \mathrm{d}\vec{x} \tag{4.8}
$$

We may obtain expressions for these derivative terms by referring to Eq. (4.3) and expanding the triple summation over (i, j, k) to produce the 64×1 vector:

$$
\gamma^{(\delta_x, \delta_y, \delta_z)} = \begin{bmatrix} (Q_x^{(\delta_x)}(0, a)\vec{x}(a))(Q_y^{(\delta_y)}(0, b)\vec{y}(b))(Q_z^{(\delta_z)}(0, c)\vec{z}(c)) \\ (Q_x^{(\delta_x)}(1, a)\vec{x}(a))(Q_y^{(\delta_y)}(0, b)\vec{y}(b))(Q_z^{(\delta_z)}(0, c)\vec{z}(c)) \\ \vdots \\ (Q_x^{(\delta_x)}(3, a)\vec{x}(a))(Q_y^{(\delta_y)}(3, b)\vec{y}(b))(Q_z^{(\delta_z)}(3, c)\vec{z}(c)) \end{bmatrix} \tag{4.9}
$$

leading to the expression

$$
\Gamma^{(\gamma_x, \gamma_y, \gamma_z)} = \gamma^{(\gamma_x, \gamma_y, \gamma_z)} \otimes \gamma^{(\gamma_x, \gamma_y, \gamma_z)} \tag{4.10}
$$

which allows for the production of the polynomial expressions for the squared second-order partial derivatives by setting $(\delta_x, \delta_y, \delta_z)$ and operating directly on the control-point coefficients. For example,

$$
\left(\frac{\partial^2 \nu_x}{\partial x \partial z} \right)^2 = \vec{p}_x^T \Gamma^{(1,0,1)} \vec{p}_x \text{ and } \left(\frac{\partial^2 \nu_x}{\partial x^2} \right)^2 = \vec{p}_x^T \Gamma^{(2,0,0)} \vec{p}_x \tag{4.11}
$$

We can now devise a single matrix operator for computing Eq. (4.8) over any given region supported by a set of 64 B-spline control points. Figure 4.1 provides a 2-D visualization. To later simplify computation, we separate the term Γ by B-spline basis orientation such that:

$$
\Gamma^{(\gamma_x, \gamma_y, \gamma_z)} = \Gamma^{(\gamma_x)} \otimes \Gamma^{(\gamma_y)} \otimes \Gamma^{(\gamma_z)} \tag{4.12}
$$

By separating the four rows of $Q_x^{(\delta_x)}$ into unit vectors

$$Q_x^{(\delta_x)} = \begin{bmatrix} \vec{q}_{x,0}^{\,T} \\ \vec{q}_{x,1}^{\,T} \\ \vec{q}_{x,2}^{\,T} \\ \vec{q}_{x,3}^{\,T} \end{bmatrix}^{(\delta_x)} \tag{4.13}$$

we may define the sixteen 4×4 matrices given by $\Xi_{x,a,b} = \vec{q}_{x,a} \otimes \vec{q}_{x,b}$ and construct the 4×4 matrix:

$$\Gamma_x^{(\delta_x)}(a, b) = \Xi_{x,a,b} \tag{4.14}$$

Grouping like-order polynomial terms within $\Xi_{x,a,b}$ yields the column vector:

$$\sigma_{x,a,b} = \begin{bmatrix} \Xi(0,0) \\ \Xi(0,1) + \Xi(1,0) \\ \Xi(0,2) + \Xi(1,1) + \Xi(2,0) \\ \Xi(0,3) + \Xi(1,2) + \Xi(2,1) + \Xi(3,0) \\ \Xi(1,3) + \Xi(2,2) + \Xi(3,1) \\ \Xi(2,3) + \Xi(3,2) \\ \Xi(3,3) \end{bmatrix}_{x,a,b} \tag{4.15}$$

and by integrating the resulting eighth order Cartesian bases over $\vec{r}$

$$\vec{\psi}_x = \begin{bmatrix} r_x & \frac{1}{2}r_x^2 & \frac{1}{3}r_x^3 & \frac{1}{4}r_x^4 & \frac{1}{5}r_x^5 & \frac{1}{6}r_x^6 & \frac{1}{7}r_x^7 \end{bmatrix}^T \tag{4.16}$$

the integral of $\Gamma_x^{(\delta_x)}$ over a B-spline region may be expressed as a 4×4 matrix of vector products

$$\Gamma_x^{(\delta_x)} = \int_0^{r_x} \Gamma_x^{(\delta_x)} dx = \sigma_{x,a,b}^T \vec{\psi}_x \tag{4.17}$$

and similarly for Γ_y and Γ_z. This allows for the construction of the six desired composite matrix operators

$$V^{(\delta_x, \delta_y, \delta_z)} = \begin{cases} \Gamma^{(\delta_x)} \otimes \Gamma^{(\delta_y)} \otimes \Gamma^{(\delta_z)} & \text{for } \delta_x + \delta_y + \delta_z = 1 \\ 0 & \text{otherwise} \end{cases} \tag{4.18}$$

which facilitate the rapid computation of the smoothness metric over a region indexed by (l, m, n) as

$$S_{l,m,n} = \sum_{(\delta_x, \delta_y, \delta_z)} (\vec{p}_x^T V^{(\delta_x, \delta_y, \delta_z)} \vec{p}_x + \vec{p}_y^T V^{(\delta_x, \delta_y, \delta_z)} \vec{p}_y + \vec{p}_z^T V^{(\delta_x, \delta_y, \delta_z)} \vec{p}_z) \quad (4.19)$$

and the derivative with respect to a B-spline control-point $P_{i,j,k}$ is

$$\frac{\partial S_{l,m,n}}{\partial P_{i,j,k}} = \sum_{(\delta_x, \delta_y, \delta_z)} (2 V^{(\delta_x, \delta_y, \delta_z)} \vec{p}_x + 2 V^{(\delta_x, \delta_y, \delta_z)} \vec{p}_y + 2 V^{(\delta_x, \delta_y, \delta_z)} \vec{p}_z) \quad (4.20)$$

The total penalty S and its gradient are expressible via the summations

$$S = \sum_{(l,m,n)} S_{l,m,n} \text{ and } \frac{\partial S}{\partial P_{i,j,k}} = \sum_{l=0}^{3} \sum_{m=0}^{3} \sum_{n=0}^{3} \frac{\partial S_{l,m,n}}{\partial P_{i,j,k}} \quad (4.21)$$

where the summation for S indexed by (l, m, n) is over all regions and the summation for the gradient is over the 64 regions within the local support of the control point $P_{i,j,k}$.

4.3 ALGORITHMIC IMPLEMENTATION

Because the set of six matrix operators $V^{(\delta_x, \delta_y, \delta_z)}$ depend only on the B-spline grid configuration, they may be precomputed before the registration begins and simply reused within each iteration. Therefore, the algorithmic implementation of the regularization process consists of two stages: an initialization stage and an update stage. During the initialization stage, the six matrix operators are simply constructed and stored. The update stage occurs at the end of each optimization iteration and consists of applying the precomputed matrix operators to the B-spline coefficients in order to compute the vector field smoothness S and its derivative with respect to each control point $\partial S/\partial P$. This stage concludes by adding the smoothness S to the overall cost function C as in Eq. (4.2) and the smoothness derivative $\partial S/\partial P$ to the cost-function gradient $\partial C/\partial P$ as per Eq. (5.3).

First we consider the initialization process, which is performed along with all other B-spline initialization procedures. Only the B-spline control-point spacing in each spatial dimension is required for generation of the six $V^{(\delta_x, \delta_y, \delta_z)}$ matrix operators. This initialization process is

```
1: /* Generate the Q matrices from (4.5) through (4.7) */
2: Q_x^(0) = BR_x
3: Q_y^(0) = BR_y
4: Q_z^(0) = BR_z
5:
6: /* Generate first and second derivatives as in (4.5) through (4.7) */
7: Q_x^(1) = Q_x^(0) Δ^(1)
8: Q_y^(1) = Q_y^(0) Δ^(1)
9: Q_z^(1) = Q_z^(0) Δ^(1)
10: Q_x^(2) = Q_x^(0) Δ^(2)
11: Q_y^(2) = Q_y^(0) Δ^(2)
12: Q_z^(2) = Q_z^(0) Δ^(2)
13:
14: /* Generate Γ̄_x^(0), Γ̄_x^(1), Γ̄_x^(2) as per (4.13) through (4.17) */
15: Γ̄_x^(0) = eval_integral(Q_x^(0), r_x)
16: Γ̄_x^(1) = eval_integral(Q_x^(1), r_x)
17: Γ̄_x^(2) = eval_integral(Q_x^(2), r_x)
18:
19: /* Generate Γ̄_y^(0), Γ̄_y^(1), Γ̄_y^(2) as per (4.13) through (4.17) */
20: Γ̄_y^(0) = eval_integral(Q_y^(0), r_y)
21: Γ̄_y^(1) = eval_integral(Q_y^(1), r_y)
22: Γ̄_y^(2) = eval_integral(Q_y^(2), r_y)
23:
24: /* Generate Γ̄_z^(0), Γ̄_z^(1), Γ̄_z^(2) as per (4.13) through (4.17) */
25: Γ̄_z^(0) = eval_integral(Q_z^(0), r_z)
26: Γ̄_z^(1) = eval_integral(Q_z^(1), r_z)
27: Γ̄_z^(2) = eval_integral(Q_z^(2), r_z)
28:
29: /* Generate V_1 through V_6 as per (4.18) */
30: V_1 = Γ̄_x^(2) ⊗ Γ̄_y^(0) ⊗ Γ̄_z^(0)
31: V_2 = Γ̄_x^(0) ⊗ Γ̄_y^(2) ⊗ Γ̄_z^(0)
32: V_3 = Γ̄_x^(0) ⊗ Γ̄_y^(0) ⊗ Γ̄_z^(2)
33: V_4 = Γ̄_x^(1) ⊗ Γ̄_y^(1) ⊗ Γ̄_z^(0)
34: V_5 = Γ̄_x^(1) ⊗ Γ̄_y^(0) ⊗ Γ̄_z^(1)
35: V_6 = Γ̄_x^(0) ⊗ Γ̄_y^(1) ⊗ Γ̄_z^(1)
```

Figure 4.2 Initializing the regularizer by constructing the various matrix operators.

described algorithmically in Figures 4.2 and 4.3. Lines 1−4 normalize the B-spline basis by the control-grid spacing for each Cartesian axis as per Eq. (4.5). This is necessary so that any given voxel coordinate within a tile will be normalized within [0,1], the range within which the B-spline basis functions are defined. Lines 6−12 generate the first- and second-order spatial derivatives of the normalized B-spline basis functions as per Eq. (4.7). Lines 14−17 generate the matrices $\Gamma_x^{(0)}, \Gamma_x^{(1)}$, and $\Gamma_x^{(2)}$ by squaring Eq. (4.2) for the zeroth-, first-, and second-order normalized B-spline basis functions $Q_x^{(0)}, Q_x^{(1)}$, and $Q_x^{(2)}$, respectively, by and

```
1: function eval_integral(Q, r)
2:    for λ₂ = 0 to 3 step 1
3:       for λ₁ = 0 to 3 step 1
4:          /* As per (4.13) */
5:          Ξ = q⃗(λ₁) ⊗ q⃗(λ₂)
6:
7:          /* As per (4.14) through (4.17) */
8:          Γ̄(λ₁, λ₂) = (r¹/1)(Ξ(0,0))
9:                     + (r²/2)(Ξ(0,1) + Ξ(1,0))
10:                    + (r³/3)(Ξ(0,2) + Ξ(1,1) + Ξ(2,0))
11:                    + (r⁴/4)(Ξ(0,3) + Ξ(1,2) + Ξ(2,1) + Ξ(3,0))
12:                    + (r⁵/5)(Ξ(1,3) + Ξ(2,2) + Ξ(3,1))
13:                    + (r⁶/6)(Ξ(2,3) + Ξ(3,2))
14:                    + (r⁷/7)(Ξ(3,3))
15:       end for
16:    end for
17:
18:    return Γ̄
19: end function
```

Figure 4.3 Generation of the integrated sub-matrices Γ.

integrating the resulting 6th order polynomials over the control-point spacing in the x-direction as per Eqs. (4.14)–(4.17). Similarly, this operation is performed in the y and z directions to obtain $\Gamma_y^{(0)}, \Gamma_y^{(1)}, \Gamma_y^{(2)}, \Gamma_z^{(0)}, \Gamma_z^{(1)}$, and $\Gamma_z^{(2)}$. This process of squaring and integrating is performed within the function eval_integral(), which is algorithmically described in Figure 4.3. Finally, lines 29−35 complete the initialization process by computing the six $V^{(\delta_x, \delta_y, \delta_z)}$ matrices via the tensor product as per Eq. (4.18).

Once the six $V^{(\delta_x, \delta_y, \delta_z)}$ matrix operators are obtained, the smoothness S and its derivative $\partial S / \partial P$ may be quickly computed for any given tile via Eqs. (4.19) and (4.20). Figures 4.4 and 4.5 describe the process of computing the smoothness for the entire vector field by sequentially computing the vector field smoothness for each tile $S_{l,m,n}$ and accumulating the results as in Eq. (4.21). For each iteration we first use the tile's index tile_index to compute the indices of the 64 control points that are associated with that tile. These indices are stored into the 64 element array cp_lut as shown in line 4. The remainder of the iteration computes the smoothness of the individual tile's vector field by applying the six $V^{(\delta_x, \delta_y, \delta_z)}$ matrix operators as shown in lines 7−12 in Figure 4.4 and summing the results.

```
 1: S = 0
 2: for tile_idx = 0 to NUM_TILES-1 step 1
 3:     /* Generate array containing indices for tile's 64 control points */
 4:     cp_lut = find_control_points(tile_idx)
 5:
 6:     /* Sum partial derivatives as per (4.19) and (4.20) */
 7:     S += apply_operator(cp_lut, V₁)
 8:     S += apply_operator(cp_lut, V₂)
 9:     S += apply_operator(cp_lut, V₃)
10:     S += apply_operator(cp_lut, V₄)
11:     S += apply_operator(cp_lut, V₅)
12:     S += apply_operator(cp_lut, V₆)
13: end for
```

Figure 4.4 The update stage of the regularizer that computes the smoothness for the entire vector field.

```
 1: function apply_operator(cp_lut, V)
 2:     for j = 0 to 63 step 1
 3:         /* Compute tile smoothness as per (4.19). */
 4:         for i = 0 to 63 step 1
 5:             tmp_x[j] += P[3*cp_lut[i]+0] * V[64*j+i]
 6:             tmp_y[j] += P[3*cp_lut[i]+1] * V[64*j+i]
 7:             tmp_z[j] += P[3*cp_lut[i]+2] * V[64*j+i]
 8:         end for
 9:
10:         Stile += tmp_x[j] * P[3*cp_lut[i]+0]
11:         Stile += tmp_y[j] * P[3*cp_lut[i]+1]
12:         Stile += tmp_z[j] * P[3*cp_lut[i]+2]
13:         /* --------------------------------------- */
14:
15:         /* Compute tiles smoothness derivative as per (4.20). */
16:         ∂C/∂P[3*cp_lut[j]+0] += 2 * λ * tmp_x[j]
17:         ∂C/∂P[3*cp_lut[j]+1] += 2 * λ * tmp_y[j]
18:         ∂C/∂P[3*cp_lut[j]+2] += 2 * λ * tmp_z[j]
19:     end for
20:
21:     return Stile
22: end function
```

Figure 4.5 The regularization operation applied to the B-spline coefficients.

For subsequent iterations we continue to accumulate into S, thereby computing the smoothness for the entire vector field as prescribed by Eq. (4.21).

Figure 4.5 details the steps involved in applying the $V^{(\delta_x, \delta_y, \delta_z)}$ matrix operators to a set of 64 control points. Here, lines 4−12 implement the straightforward matrix multiplication required by the $\vec{p}_x^T V \vec{p}_x$

operation found in Eq. (4.19). The array V[ ] holds the 64×64 matrix operator being applied to the B-spline coefficients stored within P[ ], which is x, y, z-interlaced. The control-point index lookup table cp_lut passed into the function contains the indices of the 64 control points for the tile in question; thus its use in lines 5−7 and 10−12 serves as a means of converting from tile-centric control-point indexing (ranging from 0 to 63) to the absolute control-point indexing used within the B-spline coefficient array P[ ]. Furthermore, due to the operational similarity found in the computation of the tile smoothness $S_{l,m,n}$ and its derivative $\partial S_{l,m,n}/\partial P$, we are able to compute Eq. (4.20) in place using the partial solutions tmp_x[ ], tmp_y[ ], and tmp_z[ ] from the tile smoothness computations as shown in lines 16−18.

Finally, it should be noted that since the computation of an individual tile's smoothness is independent of all other tiles, it is possible to parallelize the algorithm by simply spreading the iterations of Figure 4.4 across N cores and performing a sum reduction on the resulting N values of S. Additionally, because lines 16−18 of Figure 4.5 attempt to update 64 control-point $\partial C/\partial P$ values by appending λ weighted $\partial S/\partial P$ values as in Eq. (4.1), the cost-function gradient update operations must be modified to be thread safe. For this, the same thread-safe parallel method from Chapters 2 and 3 used to update the set of 64 $\partial C/\partial P$ values given a tile of $\partial C/\partial v$ values may be employed due to the identical data structures used in the operation with the only difference being that the $\partial S/\partial P$ data values replace the $\partial C/\partial v$ values.

4.4 PERFORMANCE EVALUATION

This section presents experimental results obtained for single- and multi-core CPU implementations in terms of both execution speed and registration quality. A numerical central differencing implementation that computes the vector field smoothness by operating directly on the vector field is provided as a basis for comparison. All implementations are evaluated in terms of execution speed as a function of (i) volume size given a fixed control-point grid and (ii) control-point spacing given a fixed volume size. Additionally, the processing time incurred for a single tile as a function of the tile's size is also investigated. As previously described, the sequential analytic implementation computes the smoothness by applying the six $V^{(\delta_x, \delta_y, \delta_z)}$ matrix operators to the B-spline coefficients pertaining to each tile—one tile at a time until all tiles within the volume are processed. Since the computation of each individual tile's smoothness is independent of other tiles, the parallel analytic implementations may process the smoothness for N tiles in parallel given N cores. Additionally, this implementation uses the parallel gradient update method developed in Chapters 2 and 3 to further accelerate the algorithm. These analytic implementations provide an interesting contrast to the numerical method of smoothness computation, which is based on central differencing of the raw vector field values at each individual voxel in the volume. Consequently, the numerical method differs from the analytic method in that it is voxel resolution centric and not control-grid resolution centric. This results in the two methods having not only differing processing speeds but fundamentally different execution-time profiles with respect to the various input parameters.

Lastly, we demonstrate the effectiveness of regularization for a multimodal case requiring the registration of an intraoperative CT to a preoperative MRI. Warped moving images with and without regularization are shown as well as their associated deformation vector field transforms. Additionally, post-warp CT-MRI fusion images are provided in order to more clearly demonstrate the affects of regularization on registration solution convergence. The tests reported here were performed using a machine equipped with an Intel quad-core i7 920 processor with each core clocked at 2.6 GHz.

4.4.1 Registration Quality

Figure 4.6 shows axial cross sections of thoracic image volumes involved in an MRI to CT multimodal registration using mutual information. CT images are shown in blue and MRI images are shown in red. Figure 4.6A is a cross section of the CT volume serving as the fixed image. Similarly, Figure 4.6B is a cross section of the MRI serving as the moving image. Figure 4.6C shows the result of a carefully conducted five-stage multiresolution B-spline grid registration that does not impose any regularization on the deformation vector field. Figure 4.6D shows the same registration that imposes the smoothness penalty term with a weight of $\lambda = 5 \times 10^{-6}$. Figure 4.7A shows the unwarped MRI image superimposed upon the CT image prior to deformable registration. As shown, the two images have been rigidly

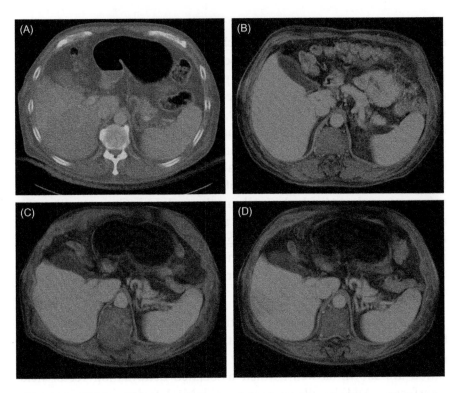

Figure 4.6 Warped thoracic images with and without regularization. (A) The static CT image, (B) the moving MRI image, (C) the warped MRI after registration without regularization, and (D) the warped MRI after registration with a regularization factor of $\lambda = 5 \times 10^{-6}$.

registered manually to one another such that the common vertebra is aligned. Notice the significant liver deformation on the left of the thorax and the spleen deformation found on the right posterior. The aim of the deformable registration is to recover the deformation vector field accurately describing the movement of these organs and surrounding dynamic anatomy.

We will first analyze the registration result in Figure 4.7 without regularization. Despite this deformation being physically impossible, as we will show, it does meet the mutual information criteria for a good registration. Consequently, the fusion of this solution with the fixed CT image is visually favorable as shown in Figure 4.7B. However, notice how the MRI image warped by the unregularized vector field, when viewed by itself in Figure 4.6C appears "wavy" and exhibits artifacting reminiscent of a thin film of oil—particularly pronounced within the spinal column and the anterior layer of fat around the

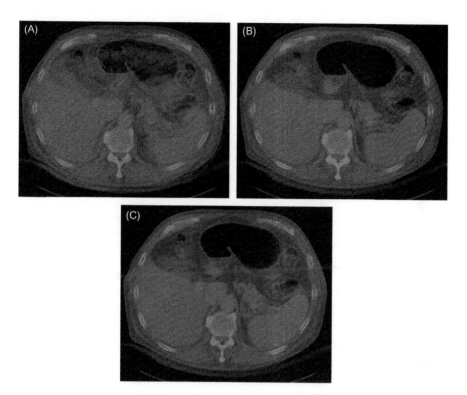

Figure 4.7 Fusion of MRI and CT thoracic images with and without regularization. (A) The original MRI image superimposed on the CT image, (B) the MRI warped without regularization and superimposed on the CT, and (C) the MRI warped with regularization and superimposed on the CT.

abdomen. Naturally, the human body is incapable of deforming in this fashion and direct inspection of the deformation field shown in Figure 4.8A confirms its implausibility.

In contrast, Figure 4.6D shows the result for the same registration performed with a regularization penalty weight of $\lambda = 5 \times 10^{-6}$. Notice how the artifacting is no longer present—the deformation appears physically sane; accordingly, the deformation vector field shown in Figure 4.8B confirms that the mapping is sane. Finally, the superimposition of this warped MRI upon the reference CT image shown in Figure 4.7C represents an accurate anatomical correlation between the intraoperative CT and the preoperative MRI images.

4.4.2 Sensitivity to Volume Size

This set of tests characterizes each implementation's sensitivity, in terms of execution time, to increasing volume size where the volumes

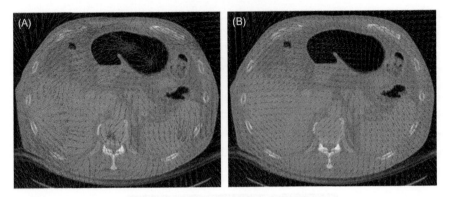

Figure 4.8 Multimodal vector fields with and without regularization. (A) Superimposed position of a 2-D slice of a 3-D deformation vector field upon the corresponding axial thoracic CT slice. This vector field was generated from an MRI to CT registration that did not employ regularization. (B) Superimposition of a vector field upon a CT image that underwent the same registration but with a regularization penalty weight of $\lambda = 5 \times 10^{-6}$.

are synthetically generated. We fix the control-point spacing at 15 voxels in each physical dimension and increase the volume size in steps of $5 \times 5 \times 5$ voxels. For each volume size, we record the execution time incurred by a single iteration of the regularization process. Figure 4.9A summarizes the results. As expected for the numerically derived solution, the execution time increases linearly with the number of voxels involved. Figure 4.9B shows the same graph excluding the numerical method. Notice how the execution time for the analytic method increases only when the volume size increases by an integer multiple of the control-point grid spacing. This is because the analytic algorithm operates directly on the control-point coefficients in order to compute the vector field smoothness for a tile. Therefore, the execution time depends only on the number of tiles within the volume. Increasing the volume size by a multiple of the control-point spacing introduces additional tiles, incurring additional overall processing time for the volume. In the case of a large test volume of $500 \times 500 \times 500$ voxels, the single-core analytic implementation exhibits a speedup of 191 times over the numerical method. For the same volume size, the parallel analytic method achieves an additional $3.2x$ speedup—a speedup of $613x$ with respect to the numerical method.

4.4.3 Sensitivity to Control-Point Spacing
Figure 4.10A shows the execution time for all three regularizer implementations over a single registration iteration as a function of control-point grid spacing with the volume size held constant at

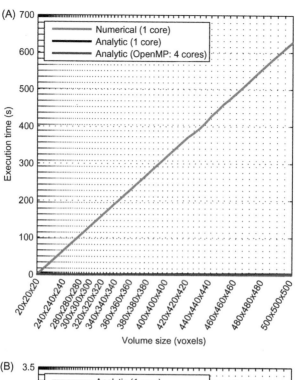

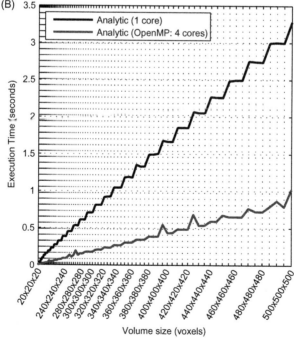

Figure 4.9 Performance of the regularizer with respect to volume size. (A) Execution times for each regulariza-tion implementation as a function of input volume size. Control-point spacing is fixed at $5 \times 5 \times 5$ voxels. (B) Only showing analytic implementations.

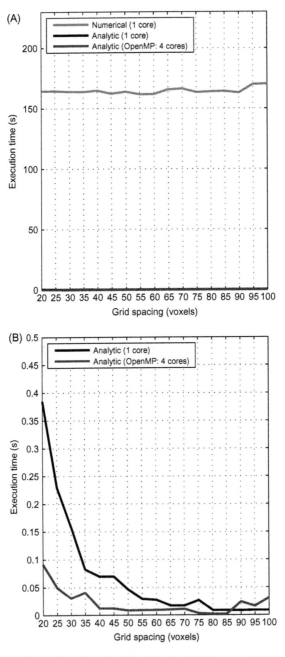

Figure 4.10 Performance of the regularizer with respect to the control-grid spacing. (A) The execution times for each regularization implementation as a function of control-point grid size. The input volume size is fixed at 320 × 320 × 320 voxels. (B) Showing the performance of only the analytic implementations.

$320 \times 320 \times 320$ voxels. As explained, the execution time for the numerical implementation is agnostic to the control-point spacing since it performs central differencing at every point in the vector field. Figure 4.10B shows the execution times incurred by just the analytically derived solutions. Interestingly, the analytic implementations exhibit an inverse cubic decay in execution time with respect to control-point spacing, with finer spacings incurring longer execution times. This phenomenon is most easily explained by examining the execution time required to compute the smoothness for a single tile with respect to tile size as shown in Figure 4.11. As shown in Figure 4.11B, as the tile size increases, the time required for the analytic implementations to process that tile remains constant. This is because the computation operation is based only on the coefficients of the 64 control points which define the tile. If the spacing between these 64 control points increase, the number of elements required to perform the computation remains unchanged—only the B-spline normalization matrices R_x, R_y, and R_z from Eq. (4.6) are modified, which has no effect on processing time. Consequently, the inverse cubic execution profile exhibited by the analytic algorithms in Figure 4.10B is due only to the number of tiles decreasing in each of the three spatial volume dimensions as the control-point spacing is isometrically increased. Finally, Figure 4.11A shows the execution time to increase with tile size for the central differencing-based numerical algorithm. However, because this algorithm's processing time is solely dependent on the total number of voxels in the image volume, the overall execution time remains unchanged with control-point spacing as shown in Figure 4.10A. In other words, if the volume holds constant dimensionality, increase the control-point spacing results in longer processing times per tile, however the number of tiles have proportionally decreased; thus resulting in an overall unchanged processing time for the image volume as a whole.

4.5 SUMMARY

We have developed an analytic method for computing the smoothness of a vector deformation field parameterized by uniform cubic B-spline basis coefficients. Furthermore, we have demonstrated how to integrate this smoothness metric into the deformable registration workflow; thereby constraining the solution of the vector deformation field and regularizing the ill-posedness of the image registration problem.

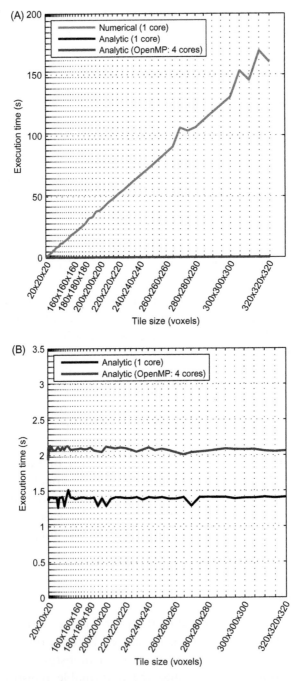

Figure 4.11 Performance of the regularizer with respect to tile size. (A) Execution times for each regularizer implementation as a function of tile size. For these tests, only the time to process a single tile is measured. (B) Showing the performance of only the analytic implementations.

The effectiveness of this method of regularization has been validated by performing multimodal MI-based deformable registration of a preoperative thoracic MRI to an intraoperational thoracic CT scan. The warped images, fused images, and vector field visualizations show increased anatomical correctness for registration procedures incorporating regularization over otherwise identical procedures excluding regularization. Finally, performance analysis shows our analytic method for computing the smoothness metric to be independent of volume resolution and 191 times faster than the traditional numerical method of computation based on central differencing—reducing the operation from hundreds of seconds to approximately 1 s for most registration configurations. By parallelizing the analytic algorithm via OpenMP, we achieved a speed up of over 3.2 times the single-core analytic algorithm when executed on a four core Intel i7 920 processor; thus providing sub-second processing times for even the most demanding medical image registration problems.

REFERENCES

Chun, S.Y., Fessler, J.A., Kessler, M.L., 2009. A simple penalty that encourages local invertibility and considers sliding effects for respiratory motion. Proc. SPIE7259, Medical Imaging: Image Processing 72592U, Lake Buena Vista, FL, USA.

Li, X., Dawant, B., Welch, E., Chakravarthy, A., Freehardt, D., Mayer, I., et al., 2009. A nonrigid registration algorithm for longitudinal breast MR images and the analysis of breast tumor response. Magn. Reson. Imaging 27 (9), 1258–1270.

Miller, M., Christensen, G., Amit, Y., Grenander, U., 1993. Mathematical textbook of deformable neuroanatomies. Proc. Natl Acad. Sci. USA. 90 (24), 11944–11948.

Ruhling, T., Maurer Jr, C., Bluemke, D., Jacobs, M., 2003. Volume-preserving nonrigid registration of MR breast images using free-form deformation with an incompressibility constraint. IEEE Trans. Med. Imaging 22 (6), 730–741.

Rueckert, D., Sonoda, L., Hayes, C., Hill, D., Leach, M., Hawkes, D., 1999. Nonrigid registration using free-form deformations: application to breast MR images. IEEE Trans. Med. Imaging 18 (8), 712–721.

CHAPTER 5

Deformable Registration Using Optical-Flow Methods

Information in This Chapter:
- Demons algorithm for deformable registration
- GPU-based version of demons algorithm
- Performance results

5.1 INTRODUCTION

This chapter develops a data-parallel model for the "demons" algorithm, a well-known deformable registration method based on optical flow (Horn and Schunck, 1981). In general, optical-flow methods describe the registration problem as a set of flow equations under the assumption that image intensities are constant between views. The demons algorithm is a variant of this approach which combines a stabilized vector-field estimation algorithm with Gaussian regularization (Thirion, 1998). It is iterative and alternates between solving the flow equations and regularization.

Demons registration is a good candidate for GPU-based acceleration due to the significant amount of fine-grain parallelism that can be extracted from the algorithm; the flow equations can be evaluated at each individual voxel in parallel and so can the smoothing procedure (Gu et al., 2010; Samant et al., 2008; Sharp et al., 2007). Samant et al. develop and benchmark a CUDA version of the demons algorithm on the Nvidia 8800 GTX GPU, reporting a speedup of about 30 times over a multithreaded implementation using two threads on a 2.4 GHz Intel CPU. Gu et al. implement both the basic version of the demons algorithm and five additional variants in CUDA to determine the algorithm(s) with the best performance in terms of both accuracy and efficiency. The algorithms are used in the context of a multiresolution registration workflow for adaptive radiotherapy applications. The authors also benchmark the algorithms using a Nvidia 285 GTX GPU and report a speedup of 40 times over a 2.3 GHz Intel Xeon processor.

High-Performance Deformable Image Registration Algorithms for Manycore Processors.
DOI: http://dx.doi.org/10.1016/B978-0-12-407741-6.00005-0

We describe a data-parallel design for the demons deformable registration algorithm that develops both the flow equations and the regularizer within the SIMD model. The GPU version is implemented
using CUDA on the Nvidia 680 GTX GPU and its performance is
analyzed in terms of speed and accuracy using CT data of a preserved
swine lung. Our results indicate substantial speedup of 150 times for
large volumes (e.g., 250^3 voxels) over a single-threaded CPU reference
implementation executed on an Intel Core i7-3770 CPU clocked at
3.40 GHz. Also, comparing the accuracy of CPU and GPU implementations, the RMS differences were less than 0.1 mm for the vector field
generated for deformable registration.

5.2 DEMONS ALGORITHM FOR DEFORMABLE REGISTRATION

Optical-flow methods describe the registration problem as a set of flow
equations under the assumption that image intensities are constant
between views. The most common variant, especially that used in medical applications, is the "demons algorithm," which combines a stabilized vector-field estimation algorithm with Gaussian regularization.
The algorithm is iterative and alternates between solving the flow
equations and regularization.

Let us consider two time-lapse images M and S, where M denotes
the moving image and S the static image. For a given voxel, let m and
s be its intensities within M and S, respectively. The theoretic basis of
optical flow follows from an assumption that the intensity of a moving
object (from M to S) is constant with time, which, for small displace-
ments, gives the optical-flow equation

$$\vec{\nu}.\vec{\nabla}s = m - s \qquad (5.1)$$

where $\vec{\nabla}s$ denotes the brightness gradient within the image S (Horn
and Schunck, 1981). Here, $\vec{\nu}$ denotes the velocity of the voxel in the
(x, y, z) space since the images correspond to two successive time
frames; $\vec{\nu}$ can also be considered as the displacement of the voxel during the time interval between the two image frames.

The goal is to solve for the displacement vector $\vec{\nu}$ for each voxel.
Since Eq. (5.1) is under-constrained, a minimum-norm constraint can
be applied to yield a solution for the optical flow. However, the flow
will be unstable in regions where the image gradient ∇s is very small,

leading to a very large (even infinite) value for $\vec{\nu}$. Therefore, to correct this problem, Thirion stabilized the vector-field estimation by underestimating the displacement at locations where the image gradient is small (Thirion, 1998); to compensate for this, Gaussian regularization (or smoothing) is applied to the vector field to fill in those regions that are underestimated.

The following equations are solved for each voxel and make up the overall demons algorithm.

$$\vec{\nu}_0 = 0 \tag{5.2}$$

$$\vec{\nu}'_k = \vec{\nu}_{k-1} + \frac{(m-s)\vec{\nabla}s}{(\vec{\nabla}s)^2 + (m-s)^2} \tag{5.3}$$

$$\vec{\nu}_k = \text{smooth}\,(\vec{\nu}'_k) \tag{5.4}$$

During each iteration k, Eq. (5.3) obtains a preliminary estimate of the displacement $\vec{\nu}'_k$ for each voxel using the spatial gradient of image intensities $\vec{\nabla}s$ and the image-intensity difference $m-s$. However, if $(\vec{\nabla}s)^2 + (m-s)^2$ in the denominator of Eq. (5.3) is too small, then the equation is unstable and $\vec{\nu}'_k$ is not changed. Next, the displacement field is regularized using a Gaussian smoothing filter in Eq. (5.4), ensuring that displacement estimates diffuse out from regions having strong image gradients to regions with weak gradients. This optical-flow process is repeated for the number of iterations needed for $\vec{\nu}$ to converge usually between 50 and 100 iterations.

If k iterations are performed on a volume of m^3 voxels, and if the size of the smoothing kernel is small, the demons algorithm has a computational complexity of $O(km^3)$. The computations of $m-s$ and $\vec{\nabla}s$ can be performed independently for each voxel and therefore can be parallelized. So, if there are p processors, the complexity is $O(km^3/p)$.

5.3 SIMD VERSION OF DEMONS ALGORITHM

As discussed in the earlier section, the demons algorithm for deformable registration is iterative and alternates between the computationally intensive tasks of updating the velocity vector field and Gaussian regularization. We show how to develop kernels to: (1) compute the intensity gradient of an image $\vec{\nabla}s$; (2) estimate the displacement-vector field using Eq. (5.3); and (3) regularize the vector field via separable Gaussian filters (Eq. (5.4)).

Figure 5.1 lists a snippet of the CUDA code executed on the CPU to calculate the deformation field using the demons algorithm. Lines 5−9

```
void demons_host_code(Volume *S, Volume *M, Volume *result, int num_iter){
1.      float3 dim = (S->dim[0], S->dim[1], S->dim[2]);            // The (x, y, z) dimensions of the volume
2.      float3 spacing = (S->spacing[0], S->spacing[1], S->spacing[2]);   // Dimensions of each voxel
3.      float vol_size = M->dim[0] * M->dim[1] * M->dim[2] * sizeof(float);   // Size of the volume in bytes
4.      float interleaved_vol_size = 3 * S->dim[0] * S->dim[1] * S->dim[2] * sizeof(float); // Size of interleaved volume

        /* Set up the execution grid on the GPU. */
5.      int threadX = BLOCK_SIZE;   int threadY = 1;   int threadZ = 1;
6.      int blockX = (S->dim[0] + threadX - 1) / threadX;
7.      int blockY = (S->dim[1] + threadY - 1) / threadY;
8.      int blockZ = (S->dim[2] + threadZ - 1) / threadZ;
9.      dim3 block = dim3(threadX, threadY, threadZ);   dim3 grid = dim3(blockX, blockY * blockZ);

        /* Allocate and copy the necessary data structures to GPU memory. Bind the fixed image volume S and the moving
           image volume M to GPU texture memory. Copy the dim and spacing data structures to GPU constant memory.
           Code is omitted for brevity. */

        /* Kernel call to compute the gradient of the moving image; the resulting volume is strored in d_m_grad. */
10.     gradient_kernel<<< grid, block>>>(d_m_grad, blockY);
11.     cudaBindTexture(0, tex_grad, d_m_grad, interleaved_vol_size); // Bind the gradient volume to GPU texture

        /* Calculate magnitude of the gradient vector at each voxel and bind the resulting volume to texture. */
12.     gradient_magnitude_kernel<<< grid, block>>> (d_m_grad_mag, blockY);
13.     cudaBindTexture (0, tex_grad_mag, d_m_grad_mag, vol_size);

14.     /* Create the separable smoothing kernels for (x, y, z) directions and copy them to GPU constant memory. */

        /* Obtain the vector field in iterative fashion. */
15.     for(int i = 0; i < num_iter; i++){
16.         cudaBindTexture(0, tex_vf_smooth, d_vf_smooth, interleaved_vol_size);
17.         estimate_kernel<<< grid, block >>> (d_vf_est, denominator_eps, blockY);

            /* Smooth the estimate into vf_smooth. The volumes are ping-ponged. */
18.         cudaUnbindTexture(tex_vf_smooth); cudaBindTexture(0, tex_vf_est, d_vf_est, interleaved_vol_size);
19.         vf_convolve_x_kernel<<< grid, block >>>(d_vf_smooth, d_kerx, half_width, blockY);

20.         cudaUnbindTexture(tex_vf_est); cudaBindTexture(0, tex_vf_smooth, d_vf_smooth, interleaved_vol_size);
21.         vf_convolve_y_kernel<<< grid, block >>>(d_vf_est, d_kery, half_width, blockY);

22.         cudaUnbindTexture(tex_vf_smooth); cudaBindTexture(0, tex_vf_est, d_vf_est, interleaved_vol_size);
23.         vf_convolve_z_kernel<<< grid, block >>>(d_vf_smooth, d_kerz, half_width, blockY);

24.         d_swap = d_vf_est; d_vf_est = d_vf_smooth; d_vf_smooth = d_swap; // Ping-pong between buffers
        }

        /* Copy result back to the CPU. */
25.     cudaMemcpy (result->img, d_vf_est, interleaved_vol_size, cudaMemcpyDeviceToHost);

}
```

Figure 5.1 Snippet of the code executed on the CPU side to obtain the deformation vector field using demons registration.

set up the execution grid on the GPU. (The thread-block size, which is tunable, is set to BLOCK_SIZE = 256 threads in our experiments.) Then the static and moving images, S and M, respectively, as well as other key data structures are transferred from the CPU's memory to the GPU, and mapped to texture and constant memories. Constant memory is a type of cached memory in the GPU's memory hierarchy that can be used for data that will not change over the course of a kernel's execution. Reading from constant memory conserves memory bandwidth when compared to reading the same data from global memory. The use of constant memory has other advantages as well: a single read from constant memory can be broadcast to all threads making up a half-warp (a group of 16 threads), and since constant memory is cached, consecutive reads to the same address does not incur any additional memory traffic. Texture memory is another type of read-only memory on the GPU which like constant memory is also cached on chip. So, it can provide higher effective bandwidth by reducing memory requests to global memory. Texture caches are specifically designed for memory access patterns that exhibit spatial locality.

Returning to Figure 5.1, once the static and moving images have been transferred to the GPU, the kernel call to `gradient_kernel()` calculates the intensity gradient $\vec{\nabla}s$, denoted as `d_m_grad`, which is then bound to the texture cache (lines 10 and 11). The kernel `gradient_magnitude_kernel()` calculates the magnitude of the gradient $(\nabla s)^2$ at each voxel location, which is also cached within the texture unit (lines 12 and 13). Finally, lines 15–24 obtain the vector field in an iterative fashion by first obtaining an initial estimate `d_vf_est` via a kernel call to `estimate_kernel()` and then smoothing this estimate, also on the GPU, using three separable Gaussian kernels to obtain `d_vf_smooth`. The calculation "ping-pongs" between the `d_vf_est` and `d_vf_smooth` volumes in that if `d_vf_est` is treated as the input volume and `d_vf_smooth` as the output buffer during an iteration, the roles of these volumes are reversed in the following iteration, and so on. Also, since the various kernel calls shown in Figure 5.1 have data dependencies between them, we introduce synchronization barriers between them (using `cudaThreadSynchronize()`), which are not shown in the listing for the sake of brevity.

Figure 5.2 provides the listing for `gradient_kernel()` that computes the image-intensity gradient ∇s on the GPU using the central

```
/* The various texture mappings. */
texture<float, 1, cudaReadModeElementType> tex_fixed;        // Fixed image
texture<float, 1, cudaReadModeElementType> tex_moving;       // Moving image
texture<float, 1, cudaReadModeElementType> tex_grad;         // Image gradient
texture<float, 1, cudaReadModeElementType> tex_grad_mag;     // Magnitude of the gradient at each voxel
texture<float, 1, cudaReadModeElementType> tex_vf_est;       // Estimated vector field
texture<float, 1, cudaReadModeElementType> tex_vf_smooth;    // Smoothed vector field

/* Allocations in constant memory. */
__constant__ int dim[3];          // Dimensions of the volume in the x, y, and z dimensions
__constant__ spacing[3];          // Voxel spacing in each dimension

/* This helper function returns the linear address of the voxel (i, j, k) within the volume array. */
__device__ int volume_index(int *dims, int i, int j, int k){
        return i + (dims[0] * (j + dims[1] * k));
}

__global__ void gradient_kernel (float *out_img, unsigned int blockY){
        /* Find the 3D position (i, j, k) of the voxel within the volume. */
1.      int blockIdx_z = __float2int_rd(blockIdx.y/(float)BlockY);
2.      int blockIdx_y = blockIdx.y - blockIdx_z, * blockY;
3.      int i = blockIdx.x * blockDim.x + threadIdx.x;
4.      int j = blockIdx_y * blockDim.y + threadIdx.y;
5.      int k = blockIdx_z * blockDim.z + threadIdx.z;

6.      if (i >= dim[0] || j >= dim[1] || k >= dim[2]) return;

        /* Obtain the immediate neighbors in each dimension. Index p denotes the previous voxel, n denotes the next voxel. */
7.      int i_p = (i == 0) ? 0 : i - 1; int i_n = (i == dim[0] - 1) ? dim[0] - 1 : i + 1;
8.      int j_p = (j == 0) ? 0 : j - 1; int j_n = (j == dim[1] - 1) ? dim[1] - 1 : j + 1;
9.      int k_p = (k == 0) ? 0 : k - 1; int k_n = (k == dim[2] - 1) ? dim[2] - 1 : k + 1;

        /* Obtain the linear address of the voxel within the volume. The volume is stored in an interleaved fashion. */
10.     long v3 = 3 * ((k * dim[1] * dim[0]) + (j * dim[0]) + i);
11.     long gi = v3; long gj = v3 + 1; long gk = v3 + 2;

        /* Obtain the linear address of the immediate neighbors in each dimension; Fetch the voxel intensity values from
           texture memory and calculate the gradient at the current voxel via central differencing. */
12.     int idx_p = volume_index(dim, i_p, j, k); int idx_n = volume_index(dim, i_n, j, k);
13.     out_img[gi] = (float) (tex1Dfetch(tex_moving, idx_n) - tex1Dfetch(tex_moving, idx_p))/spacing[0];

14.     idx_p = volume_index(dim, i, j_p, k); idx_n = volume_index (dim, i, j_n, k);
15.     out_img[gj] = (float) (tex1Dfetch(tex_moving, idx_n) - tex1Dfetch(tex_moving, idx_p))/spacing[1];

16.     idx_p = volume_index(dim, i, j, k_p); idx_n = volume_index (dim, i, j, k_n);
17.     out_img[gk] = (float) (tex1Dfetch(tex_moving, idx_n) - tex1Dfetch(tex_moving, idx_p))/spacing[2];
}
```

Figure 5.2 Code listing for `gradient_kernel()` *that computes the intensity gradient at each voxel using the central differencing method.*

differencing technique. First, we find the 3D coordinates (i, j, k) of the voxel within the volume (lines 1−5) and then obtain the 3D coordinates of the six immediate neighbors to either side of this voxel (lines 7−9). The linear addresses of the immediate neighbors in each dimension are obtained; their voxel intensity values are fetched from texture memory; and the gradient is calculated at the current voxel via central differencing (lines 10−17).

```
/* Map relevant data structures to constant memory. */
__constant__ int moving_dim[3];          // Dimensions of the moving image in voxels
__constant__ float moving_spacing[3];    // Individual voxel spacing in millimeters in the moving image

__global__ void estimate_kernel (float *vf_est_img,  float denominator_eps, int blockY){
         /* Find position (i, j, k) within the volume */
1.       int blockIdx_z = __float2int_rd(blockIdx.y/(float)BlockY);
2.       int blockIdx_y = blockIdx.y - blockIdx_z * blockY;
3.       int i = blockIdx.x * blockDim.x + threadIdx.x;
4.       int j = blockIdx_y * blockDim.y + threadIdx.y;
5.       int k = blockIdx_z * blockDim.z + threadIdx.z;

6.       if (i >= dim[0] || j >= dim[1] || k >= dim[2]) return;

         /* Obtain linear address of the voxel within the volume. Recall that the volume is stored in interleaved fashion. */
7.       long fv = (k * dim[1] * dim[0]) + (j * dim[0]) + i;
8.       long f3v = 3 * fv;

         /* Find corresponding pixels (mx, my, mz) using nearest neighbor interpolation and boundary checking.
            Since the deformation vector field is specified in millimeters, we must convert the values to the corresponding
            voxel spacing. */
9.       int mz = __float2int_rn (k + tex1Dfetch(tex_vf_smooth, f3v + 2)/moving_spacing[2]);
10.      if (mz < 0 || mz >= moving_dim[2]) return;

11.      int my = __float2int_rn (j + tex1Dfetch(tex_vf_smooth, f3v + 1)/moving_spacing[1]);
12.      if (my < 0 || my >= moving_dim[1])  return;

13.      int mx = __float2int_rn (i + tex1Dfetch(tex_vf_smooth, f3v)/moving_spacing[0]);
14.      if (mx < 0 || mx >= moving_dim[0])  return;

         /* Obtain the linear address of the corresponding voxel within the moving volume. */
15.      long mv = (mz * moving_dim[1] + my) * moving_dim[0] + mx;
16.      long m3v = 3 * mv;

         /* Find the intensity difference at this correspondence between the static and moving images. */
17.      float diff = tex1Dfetch(tex_fixed, fv) - tex1Dfetch(tex_moving, mv);

18.      /* Compute denominator in Equation (5.3). */
19.      float denom = tex1Dfetch(tex_grad_mag, mv) + diff * diff;
20.      if (denom < denominator_eps) return;   // Threshold the denominator to stabilize the estimation

         /* Compute new estimate of displacement in millimeters and store the updated values in global memory. */
21.      float mult = diff / denom;
22.      vf_est_img[f3v] += mult * tex1Dfetch(tex_grad, m3v);
23.      vf_est_img[f3v + 1] += mult * tex1Dfetch(tex_grad, m3v + 1);
24.      vf_est_img[f3v + 2] += mult * tex1Dfetch(tex_grad, m3v + 2);
}
```

Figure 5.3 Code listing for estimate_kernel() that computes Eq. (5.3) for each voxel.

Figure 5.3 lists the estimate_kernel() that implements Eq. (5.3) in the demons algorithm. As with the previous kernels, lines $1-5$ obtain the (i, j, k) coordinates of the voxel within the volume. Lines 7 and 8 obtain the linear address of the voxel within the volume, recalling that the volume is stored in interleaved fashion in both global and texture memories. Lines $9-14$ find the correspondence between the static and moving images using the current vector field, that is, the corresponding pixels in M using nearest neighbor interpolation. Note that since the deformation vector field `vf_smooth` is specified in millimeters, we must convert the values to voxel spacings. Lines 15 and 16 obtain the linear address of the corresponding voxel within the moving volume and Line 17 finds the intensity difference at the correspondence between the static and moving images; the value $m - s$ specified in Eq. (5.3). Line 19 calculates $(\vec{\nabla}s)^2 + (m - s)$, the denominator in Eq. (5.3) and if this value is less than a specified threshold, line 20 ensures that the velocity vector at that voxel is not updated, thereby ensuring the stability of the updated equation. Finally, lines 21−24 complete the calculation of Eq. (5.3) and store the updated vector field in GPU global memory.

Once the initial estimate of the vector field `d_vf_est` is obtained, it is processed using convolution filters on the GPU to obtain a smoothed field `d_vf_smooth`. A 1D convolution filter is simply a scalar product of the filter weights with the input pixels within a window surrounding each of the corresponding output pixels. More specifically, given a vector v and a convolution kernel p of size n, the convolution of the ith element of the vector is given by $\sum v(i - n)p(n)$. The elements at the boundaries, that is, elements that are "outside" the vector v are treated as if they had the value zero. A separable filter for a 3D volume is a special type of filter that can be expressed as the composition of three 1D filters, one for each of the x, y, and z directions. In this scenario, the 3D convolution operation can be decomposed into three consecutive 1D convolution operations on the data, requiring far fewer multiplications for each output element compared to a traditional 3D filter.

Figure 5.4 lists the GPU-based filter that smooths the three components of the displacement vector at each voxel in the x direction; filters for the y and z directions can be developed similarly to complete the calculation of Eq. (5.4). The filter mask is stored in constant memory on the GPU for fast access. Lines 8−11 calculate the indices for the filter, appropriately clamping the values for elements at the boundaries of the volume. The vector field `d_vf_est` is cached in the texture unit, and lines 14−21 convolve each of the three components corresponding to the voxel's displacement vector in the x direction.

5.4 PERFORMANCE EVALUATION

We now present results quantifying both the speedup achieved by the GPU version of demons over the corresponding single-threaded CPU

```
/* Map the kernel mask to constant memory. */
__constant__ float ker[WIDTH];      // The width of the kernel is set to 2*half_width + 1

__global__ void vf_convolve_x_kernel (float *vf_out, float *ker, int half_width, int blockY){
        int i, i1;                   // i is the offset in the vector field
        int j, j1, j2;               // j is the index of the kernel being applied
        int d;                       // d is the vector field direction

        /* Find the voxel position within the volume. */
1.      int blockIdx_z = __float2int_rd(blockIdx.y/(float)blockY);
2.      int blockIdx_y = blockIdx.y - blockIdx_z * blockY;
3.      int x = blockIdx.x * blockDim.x + threadIdx.x;
4.      int y = blockIdx_y * blockDim.y + threadIdx.y;
5.      int z = blockIdx_z * blockDim.z + threadIdx.z;

        /* Obtain the linear address of the voxel within the volume (which is stored in an interleaved fashion). */
6.      if (x >= dim[0] || y >= dim[1] || z >= dim[2]) return;
7.      long v3 = 3 * ((z * dim[1] * dim[0]) + (y * dim[0]) + x);

        /* Compute the appropriate indices for the filter, clamping if necessary. */
8.      j1 = x - half_width; j2 = x + half_width;
9.      if (j1 < 0) j1 = 0;
10.     if (j2 >= dim[0]) j2 = dim[0] - 1;
11.     i1 = j1 - x; j1 = j1 - x + half_width; j2 = j2 - x + half_width;

        /* Convolve in the x direction for each of the three components corresponding to our voxel's displacement vector. */
14.     long index;
15.     for (d = 0; d < 3; d++) {
16.         float sum = 0.0;
17.         for (i = i1, j = j1; j <= j2; i++, j++) {
18.             index = v3 + (3 * i) + d;
19.             sum += ker[j] * tex1Dfetch(tex_vf_est, index);
            }

20.     vf_out[v3 + d] = sum;
        }
}
```

Figure 5.4 Code listing for convolve_x_kernel() *on the GPU that smooths each of the three components of the displacement vector estimated at each voxel in the* x *direction. Kernels for the* y *and* z *directions can be developed similarly.*

implementation as well as the registration quality. The CPU version is benchmarked using an Intel Core i7-3770 CPU with four SMT cores, each clocked at 3.4 GHz, and the GPU-based algorithm is timed using an Nvidia GeForce GTX 680 containing 1536 cores, each clocked at 1.1 GHz and with 2 GB of onboard memory.

The registration algorithms were tested using CT data of a preserved swine lung inflated at constant pressure (Folkert et al., 2006), obtained from an Image-guided radiation therapy (IGRT) test bed (Berbeco et al., 2004). Both the CPU and GPU versions are validated using swine-lung images that are warped by known deformations, and the registration algorithms are expected to recover these deformations.

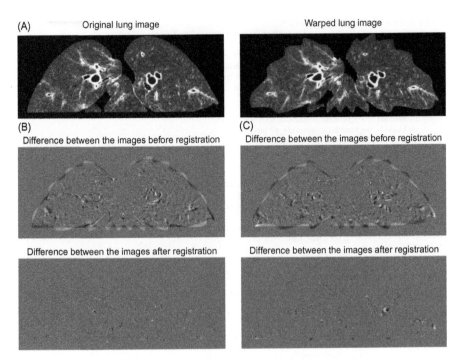

Figure 5.5 (A) The two lung images to be registered; (B) the registration results in which the warped and original lungs are the static and moving images, respectively; and (C) the registration results in which the original and warped lungs are the static and moving images, respectively.

Figure 5.5A shows the original and warped lung volumes of $424 \times 180 \times 150$ resolution to be registered, where the warping is achieved via a radially varying sinusoidal deformation. Figure 5.5B shows the registration results obtained by the GPU when the warped lung is treated as the static image and the original lungs as the moving image. Figure 5.5C shows the results assuming the original and warped lungs are now the static and moving images, respectively. This particular result as well as testing on other image sets confirms that the GPU is capable of high-quality registration with both the CPU and GPU implementations generating near-identical deformation vector fields; the RMS differences were less than 0.1 mm for the vector field generated for deformable registration.

The timing experiments performed on the CPU and GPU versions are summarized in Figure 5.6 which plots the execution time as a function of volume size (in voxels) for different widths of the smoothing kernel. The initialized vector fields are downloaded to the GPU at the

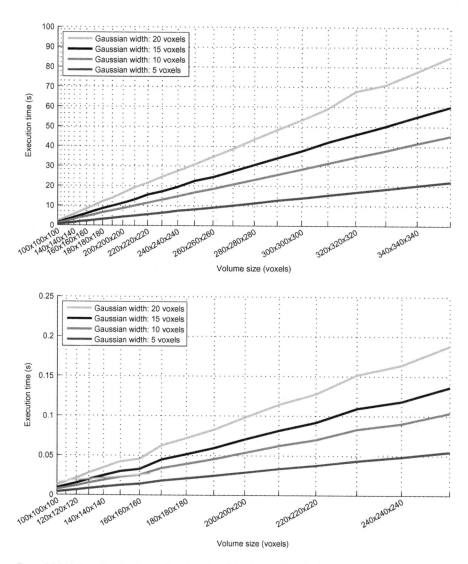

Figure 5.6 (A) Execution time incurred per iteration of the demons algorithm by a single-threaded implementation on the Intel Core i7-3770 CPU as a function of volume size and smoothing-kernel width and (B) the execution time incurred by the Nvidia 680 GTX GPU.

beginning of the registration process and read back after the specified number of iterations of the demons algorithm. Our results indicate that for larger volume sizes, the GPU achieves a substantial speedup over the serial version; for example, registering two 250^3 volumes on the CPU incurred 8 s per iteration whereas the GPU incurred 0.05 s per iteration—a speedup of about 160 times.

5.5 SUMMARY

This chapter has described the development of the demons algorithm within the SIMD programming paradigm on a GPU, implemented using CUDA and executed on the Nvidia 680 GTX GPU. Performance analysis using CT data of a preserved swine lung indicates a substantial speedup over a CPU-based reference implementation. Our results also indicate that the GPU is capable of high-quality registration with both CPU and GPU implementations generating near-identical deformation vector fields.

REFERENCES

Berbeco, R.I., Jiang, S.B., Sharp, G.C., Chen, G.T.Y., Mostafavi, H., Shirato, H., 2004. Integrated radiotherapy imaging system (IRIS): design considerations of tumor tracking with linac gantry-mounted kv x-ray systems. Phys. Med. Biol. 49 (2), 243–255.

Folkert, M., Dedual, N., Chen, G.T.Y., 2006. A biological lung phantom for {IGRT} studies. Med. Phys. 33 (6), 2234.

Gu, X., Pan, H., Liang, Y., Castillo, R., Yang, D., Choi, D., et al., 2010. Implementation and evaluation of various demons deformable image registration algorithms on a GPU. Phys. Med. Biol. 55, 207–219.

Horn, B.K.P., Schunck, B.G., 1981. Determining optical flow. Artif. Intell. 17, 185–203.

Samant, S.S., Xia, J., Muyan-Özçelik, P., Owens, J.D., 2008. High performance computing for deformable image registration: towards a new paradigm in adaptive radiotherapy. Med. Phys. 35 (8), 3546–3554.

Sharp, G., Kandasamy, N., Singh, H., Folkert, M., 2007. GPU-based streaming architectures for fast cone-beam CT image reconstruction and demons deformable registration. Phys. Med. Biol. 52 (19), 5771–5783.

Thirion, J.P., 1998. Image matching as a diffusion process: an analogy with Maxwell's demons. Med. Image Anal. 2 (3), 243–260.

CHAPTER 6

Plastimatch—An Open-Source Software for Radiotherapy Imaging

Information in This Chapter:
- Overview of Plastimatch
- Licensing

6.1 INTRODUCTION

Radiotherapy is a highly technical and rapidly changing field where increasingly sophisticated software is used to support clinical goals. Commercial software is generally high quality and is used by most clinics for routine treatment planning and delivery. However, the reliance on commercial software leaves several gaps in our ability to deliver cutting-edge treatments. When commercial software has bugs or is missing features, the clinic is required to implement complicated workarounds. Commercial software also often lacks the flexibility to communicate with complementary software from other vendors, including in-house solutions. Furthermore, it is difficult to do research with commercial medical software. Not only are vendors reluctant to provide open interfaces, but purchase and support costs are generally too high for research use. For these reasons, we expect that the role of open-source software will grow in the radiotherapy clinic.

This chapter describes the plastimatch software suite for radiotherapy image processing (Shackleford et al., 2012). Plastimatch is open-source software, distributed under a Berkeley Software Distribution (BSD)-style license. The focus of plastimatch is on high-performance algorithms for medical image computing and on flexible radiotherapy utilities. Using standard interchange formats such as DICOM and DICOM-RT, plastimatch can be easily used together with other open-source tools, including CERR (Deasy et al., 2003), Conquest DICOM (http://www.xs4all.nl/~ingenium/dicom.html), ImageJ (http://rsb.info. nih.gov/ij/), and 3D Slicer (http://slicer.org).

High-Performance Deformable Image Registration Algorithms for Manycore Processors.
DOI: http://dx.doi.org/10.1016/B978-0-12-407741-6.00006-2

6.2 OVERVIEW OF PLASTIMATCH

Plastimatch has been conceived and developed as an end-user application rather than as a library or toolkit. The standard method of using plastimatch is via the command line, with configuration files and command line options. A typical invocation would be to specify a command, such as "register," together with the necessary input files, configuration files, and options. A list of supported commands are shown in the usage screen:

```
$ plastimatch --help
plastimatch version 1.5.11-beta (3583M)
Usage: plastimatch command [options]
Commands:
```

add	adjust	average	crop	compare
compose	convert	diff	dvh	fill
header	mask	probe	register	resample
scale	segment	stats	synth	synth-vf
thumbnail	warp	xf-convert		

6.2.1 Automatic 3D–3D Registration

Plastimatch uses a multistage, multialgorithm framework for automatic image registration. Only pairwise registration is supported. In the initialization stage, the images are loaded, together with any image masks or initial transformations. The framework runs a fixed sequence of registration stages as directed by a parameter file. Each registration stage specifies the image resolution (for multiresolution registration), the transform and metric to be optimized, and the optimization algorithm and parameters. If desired, output files can be specified at each stage for saving intermediate results. A typical sequence of stages might include a single rigid alignment stage, followed by two to four deformable registration stages with increasing resolution and decreasing grid spacings. Figure 6.1 summarizes the algorithms included in plastimatch, which includes six different core registration methods. Depending on the registration method, one can choose one of four implementations: ITK, single core (SC), multicore (MC), or GPU. The six registration algorithms can operate on eight different transform types: six ITK transforms and two native transforms. At the end of each stage, the optimal transform is propagated to the next stage and is automatically converted to a new transform type by the plastimatch application framework.

Registration algorithm	ITK	SC	MC	GPU
Translation	✓			
Rigid	✓			
Affine	✓			
Demons	✓	✓		✓
B-spline (MSE, MI)	✓	✓	✓	✓
Viscous fluid				✓
Thin-plate spline	✓			
Wendland, Gaussian spline		✓		

Figure 6.1 Summary of plastimatch algorithms for 3D image registration.

6.2.2 Cone-Beam CT and Digitally Reconstructed Radiographs

A cone-beam CT reconstruction application is provided which implements filtered back-projection using the Feldkamp, Davis, and Kress (FDK) algorithm. Input images in either raw, pfm, or hnd format are read, filtered, and back-projected into a user-defined volume geometry. Images in raw or pfm format must be accompanied by a geometry specification file whereas files in the Varian hnd format use the geometry specified by the file header. Ramp filtering is performed on the CPU using the FFTW library (Frigo, 2005), while back-projection is performed on either the CPU or the GPU. The plastimatch digitally-reconstructed radiograph (DRR) generator implements three variants of the Siddon ray tracing method (Siddon, 1985). The fastest and most popular method uses the original exact path length method based on the intersection of rays with the image voxels. In addition, two voxel interpolation methods are included, which can be used to increase the apparent resolution of the DRR construction. Both multicore and GPU versions are available.

6.2.3 Interactive (Landmark-Based) Image Registration

While automatic registration yields acceptable results in many cases, we are often confronted with difficult registration problems where automatic registration fails. For this purpose, plastimatch includes two manual registration tools: a "global" landmark-based tool based on thin plate splines, and a tool based on radial basis functions (RBF) which allows us to make local registrations by adjusting the RBF support.

The global tool, implemented as an ITK wrapper, takes a list of corresponding points in 3D and generates a complete vector field that interpolates all of the input landmarks. This method requires a minimum of six landmarks, which are used to find a global affine

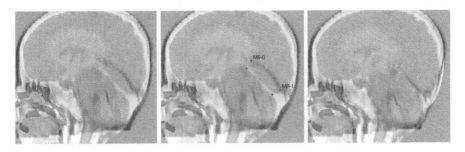

Figure 6.2 Interactive registration is used to warp the MRI of a 6-month old infant onto the CT of the same patient at age 2. The initial registration properly matches the skull, but features within the brain are not properly aligned (left). Landmarks are placed (center), which improve the registration (right).

transform superimposed with a minimum energy deformation field (Bookstein, 1989). The global landmark registration results can be used as a standalone method or to initialize the automatic registration. On the other hand, the RBF tool is a native warper and does not perform global rigid or affine mapping. Instead, it uses a small number of landmark pairs to correct failed deformable registration results. The algorithm utilizes two types of RBFs: a Wendland function with finite support (Arad and Reisfeld, 1995; Fornefett et al., 2001) and a non-truncated Gaussian function (Arad et al., 1994; Shusharina and Sharp, 2012). In both cases, a deformation is found by solving a system of linear equations which is computationally very efficient when compared with algorithms based on complex multidimensional minimization. In addition, Gaussian RBFs have a distinct feature with respect to regularization, because the regularized vector field can be solved exactly with a simple equation. An independent regularization parameter is defined to control the balance between the fidelity of the alignment of landmark pairs and the smoothness of the deformation field. An example of this idea is shown in Figure 6.2 where the failed registration (left) is corrected using two pairs of landmarks (center and right).

6.2.4 2D−3D Registration

The Reg23 module of plastimatch enables rigid registration of a 3D volumetric image (e.g., a CT) with an essentially arbitrary number of projective 2D images (e.g., X-rays). The transformation parameters (three rotations and three translations) are iteratively optimized with respect to a cost function which assesses the similarity between the X-rays and on-the-fly DRRs computed from the volume. Uniform ray-casting DRR computation is implemented on the GPU using the

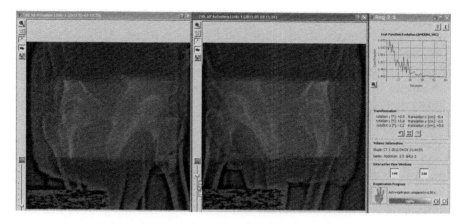

Figure 6.3 A schematic overview of the various Reg23 components (left). The Reg23 GUI showing colored over-lays of X-rays and DRRs (right). The ROI generated by the auto-masking module is shown as a blue contour. The various registration parameters are displayed in the control panel on the extreme right. (For interpretation of the references to color in this figure legend, the reader is referred to the web version of this book.)

OpenGL shading language. Besides the selected similarity metrics derived from ITK (normalized mutual information, normalized cross correlation, gradient difference, and mean reciprocal square difference), stochastic rank correlation (Steininger et al., 2010) is another configurable cost function. The input images can be preprocessed prior to registration via resampling, rescaling, cropping, or unsharp masking. Downhill simplex (AMOEBA) and 1 + 1 evolutionary algorithms are available for optimization. To restrict similarity evaluation to a certain region of interest (ROI) in the X-rays, a so-called auto-masking module is also available (Neuner et al., 2011). Based on RT structure sets which are typically generated in the preplanning stage, an entity-specific heuristic can be designed which allows logical combination, dilation/erosion, and projection of structures onto the X-ray planes which produces binary mask images that constrain metric evaluation. For example, in the case of pelvis registration, this mechanism enables automatic determination of ROIs that exclude the femora which are more prone to move, over the duration of the treatment (Steininger et al., 2012). Figure 6.3 presents a schematic overview of the main components using the example of dual 2D/3D pelvis registration. In addition to the core algorithm offering the mentioned capabilities, a Qt-based general user interface is provided as shown in Figure 6.3. The GUI enables the user to monitor the registration process and to simultaneously influence registration by mouse interactions (translation, rotation, registration, and initialization). The overall program is configurable via a simple ASCII file to enable easy integration with other applications such as record and verify systems. Also, batch processing is available where the registration results are stored in output files. We are currently working on providing more convenient means of setting up the imaging geometry, extending the portfolio of available DRR algorithms, and implementing appearance model-based 2D/3D registration.

6.2.5 Automatic Feature Detection and Matching

Several algorithms have been developed in the literature to perform automatic landmark extraction and matching, with the goal of increasing the accuracy of feature detection and decreasing the cost in terms of time. Scale Invariant Features Transform (SIFT) is a method that provides extraction and matching of stable and prominent points at different scales between two images. The algorithm, supported by Plastimatch, is derived from Cheung and Hamarneh (2009) and implemented in C++ using ITK. This method takes two 3D (isotropic or anisotropic) images as inputs and generates lists containing stable landmarks for each image as well as feature matches between the two images. The output files contain landmarks in physical coordinates that can be used with the 3D Slicer Fiducial module. Figure 6.4 shows examples of successful individuation of corresponding features in the original (left) and synthetic (right) image of a phantom (RANDO phantom, The Phantom Laboratories, Salem, NY). The synthetic image is obtained by applying rigid and nonrigid transformations to the phantom.

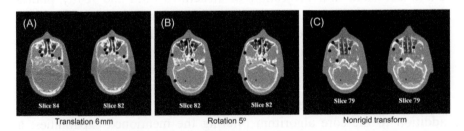

Figure 6.4 Examples of successful corresponding features detection (red codes) in the original (right) and synthetic (left) image of RANDO phantom. Rigid transforms: (A) Translation (6 mm) in right-left, anterior-posterior, superior-inferior directions and (b) rotation in superior-inferior direction. Nonrigid transform: (c) maximum deformation of 15.42, 5.72, 4.16 mm in right-left, anterior-posterior, superior-inferior directions, respectively. (For interpretation of the references to color in this figure legend, the reader is referred to the web version of this book.)

6.2.6 Data Interchange

Plastimatch supports a wide variety of file input types for data interchange. Using ITK wrappers, most image formats are supported, including DICOM, Analyze, Metaimage, and NRRD. In addition, partial support exists for DICOM-RT, XiO, and RTOG formats. Plastimatch is capable of rasterizing DICOM-RT structure sets into images, as well as converting images back into DICOM-RT structure sets. In addition, a utility is provided for attaching existing DICOM-RT structure sets onto arbitrary DICOM series.

6.2.7 User Interface

While a native user interface is supported by Reg23, the plastimatch module offers a user interface as a plugin for Aqualizer (Mori and Chen, 2008) and 3D Slicer. Aqualizer is a specialized research software for 4D treatment planning. Deformable image registration is used to map radiation dose from all breathing phases onto a reference phase, and accumulate the time-averaged dose. 3D Slicer is a general purpose research software for medical image computing and plastimatch plugins are available for automatic registration, landmark-based registration, and DICOM-RT import.

6.3 LICENSING

The plastimatch software is licensed under a BSD license for reg-2-3 and a custom BSD-style license for plastimatch. These licenses specifically allows royalty-free nonexclusive license to use, modify, and redistribute the software. The primary restrictions on licensing are that (1) attribution and copyright notices be retained, (2) modified versions must be clearly marked, and (3) names, logos, and trademarks of our institutions are not used for promotion. Our software is provided "AS IS," without warranty. The custom license clearly states that the software has been designed for research purposes only, and that clinical applications are neither recommended nor advised. A complete copy of the license is available online at http://www.plastimatch.org.

REFERENCES

Arad, N., Reisfeld, D., 1995. Image warping using few anchor points and radial functions. Comput. Graph. Forum 14 (1), 35–46.

Arad, N., Dyn, N., Reisfeld, D., Yeshurun, Y., 1994. Image warping by radial basis functions: application to facial expression. CVGIP: Graph. Models Image Process. 56 (2), 161–172.

Bookstein, F.L., 1989. Principal warps: thin-plate splines and the decomposition of deformations. IEEE Trans. Pat. Anal. Mach. Intell. 11 (6), 567−585.

Cheung, W., Hamarneh, G., 2009. n-SIFT: n-dimensional scale invariant feature transform. IEEE Trans. Image Process. 18 (9), 2012−2021.

Deasy, J.O., Blanco, A.I., Clark, V.H., 2003. CERR: a computational environment for radiotherapy research. Med. Phys. 30 (5), 979−985, <http://radium.wustl.edu/CERR>.

Fornefett, M., Rohr, K., Stiehl, H.S., 2001. Radial basis functions with compact support for elastic registration of medical images. Image Vis. Comp. 19 (1−2), 87−96.

Frigo, M., Johnson, S.G., 2005. The design and implementation of FFTW3. Proc. IEEE 93 (2), 216−231.

Mori, S., Chen, G., 2008. Quantification and visualization of charged particle range variations. Int. J. Radiat. Oncol. Biol. Phys. 72 (1), 268−277.

Neuner, M., Steininger, P., Mittendorfer, C., Sedlmayer, F., Deutschmann, H., 2011. Automatic mask generation for 2D/3D image registration with clinical images of the pelvis. Int. J. Comput. Assist. Radiol. Surg. 6 (1), S54−S55.

Shackleford, J., Shusharina, N., Verberg, J., Warmerdam, G., Winey, B., Neuner, M., et al., 2012. Plastimatch 1.6: current capabilities and future directions. MICCAI 2012 Image-Guidance and Multi-modal Dose Planning in Radiation Therapy Workshop. Nice, France.

Shusharina, N., Sharp, G., 2012. Landmark-based image registration with analytic regularization. Phys. Med. Biol. 57 (6), 1477−1498.

Siddon, R.L., 1985. Fast calculation of the exact radiological path for a three-dimensional CT array. Med. Phys. 12 (2), 252−255.

Steininger, P., Neuner, M., Birkfellner, W., Gendrin, C., Mooslechner, M., Bloch, C., et al., 2010. An ITK-based implementation of the stochastic rank correlation (SRC) metric. Insight J. July−December 2010 Issue.

Steininger, P., Neuner, M., Weichenberger, H., Sharp, G., Winey, B., Kametriser, G., et al., 2012. Auto-masked 2D/3D image registration and its validation with clinical cone-beam computed tomography. Phys. Med. Biol. 57 (13), 4277−4292.

Printed and bound by CPI Group (UK) Ltd, Croydon, CR0 4YY

03/10/2024

01040426-0011